COLOSS
PHILEMON

NCCS | New Covenant Commentary Series

This series is designed for ministers and students who require a commentary that interacts with the text and context of each New Testament book and pays specific attention to the impact of the text upon the faith and praxis of contemporary faith communities. We intend the NCCS to engage in the task of biblical interpretation and theological reflection from the perspective of the global church. The contributors come from a diverse array of backgrounds in regards to their Christian denominations and countries of origin, hailing from countries all over the world. The volumes in this series are not verse-by-verse commentaries, but instead focus on larger units of text in order to explicate and interpret the story. A further aim of these volumes is to provide an occasion for authors to reflect on how the New Testament impacts the life, faith, ministry, and witness of the New Covenant Community today. Under the heading of "Fusing the Horizons and Forming the Community", authors provide windows into community formation and ministerial formation. It is our hope that these volumes will represent serious engagements with the New Testament writings, done in the context of faith, in service of the church, and for the glorification of God.

Series Editors:

Michael F. Bird (Crossway College, Queensland, Australia)
Craig Keener (Palmer Seminary, Philadelphia, USA)

Other titles in this series:

Matthew Joel Willits
Mark Kim Huat Tan
Luke Jeannine Brown
John Jey Kanagaraj
Acts Youngmo Cho and Hyung Dae Park
Romans Craig Keener
1 Corinthians Bruce Winter
2 Corinthians David deSilva
Galatians Brian Vickers
Ephesians Lynn Cohick
Philippians Linda Belleville
1–2 Thessalonians David Garland
Pastoral Epistles Aída Besançon-Spencer
Hebrews Tom Thatcher
James Pablo Jimenez
1 Peter Eric Greaux
2 Peter and Jude Andrew Mbuvi
1–3 John Sam Ngewa
Revelation Gordon Fee

COLOSSIANS & PHILEMON

A New Covenant Commentary

MICHAEL F. BIRD

The Lutterworth Press

The Lutterworth Press
P.O. Box 60
Cambridge
CB1 2NT
United Kingdom

www.lutterworth.com
publishing@lutterworth.com

ISBN: 978 0 7188 9237 1

British Library Cataloguing in Publication Data
A record is available from the British Library

Copyright © Michael F. Bird, 2009

Published by arrangement with Cascade Books,
a division of Wipf and Stock Publishers

Contents

Preface

Commentary writing is, so I have learned, no simple feat. There is the mammoth task of doing your own translation, an immense volume of primary and secondary literature to read and interact with, and the struggle of trying to find something new or incredibly profound to say in every single verse when you find yourself most of the time agreeing with those who ploughed the textual terrain before you. I'm reminded of Calvin's words in the preface to his Romans commentary where he virtually apologizes for writing another commentary on Paul's letter despite so many fine volumes already existing:

> Since so many scholars of pre-eminent learning have previously devoted their efforts to explaining this Epistle, it seems unlikely that there is any room left for others to produce something better . . . It will, however, I hope be admitted that nothing has ever been so perfectly done by men that there is no room left for those who follow them to refine, adorn, or illustrate their work. I do not dare to say anything of myself, except that I thought that the present work would be of some profit, and that I have been led to undertake it for no other reason than the common good of the Church.

All I can say is that I have labored here as best as I can and I hope that the fruit of this work is fresh, stimulating, and challenging for those who belong to the new covenant communities of the twenty-first century. As it is, much of the content was formed through the regular delivery of sermons and in the context of worship at the Highland Theological College student chapel, where we all learned that Colossians speaks much to our contemporary age.

Colossians is my favorite book of the Pauline corpus and Philemon is a much underappreciated child of the canonical family. What links both books together I believe is the New Testament message of reconciliation. Christ is able to reconcile us to God the Father (Colossians) and he gives us the grace to be reconciled to each other (Philemon). They contain a message that our much hurting world is in desperate need of hearing. I have tried to avoid writing a commentary on other commentaries. For the most part I've started with my own translation, had an occasional glance at Jimmy Dunn's and Peter O'Brien's fine works to get some bearings, and then tackled the text myself armed with nothing but lexical aids, consulting the sundry secondary literature only after this. Done this way I believe that the commentary is much my own rather than an eclectic combination of everyone else's. In the secondary literature, I have found the works by Robin McL. Wilson, Markus Barth, Joseph Fitzmyer, N. T. Wright, Charles Talbert, Andrew Lincoln, Murray Harris, and M. M. Thompson to be the most helpful, and I certainly cannot forget to mention the pleasure of working through John Chrysostom's homilies and J. B. Lightfoot's commentary as well (how on earth did they do it without word processors and Bible software back then?).[1]

I have to thank several people for their support and assistance in the lead up to this volume. First, my co-editor Craig Keener has been a pleasure to work with. Craig has a rare combination of erudite scholarship and pastoral sensitivity. I am most grateful that Craig took a chance on working with a zany redhead Australian to launch a commentary series. His input into both this volume and the series as a whole has been priceless. Second, the editorial team at Wipf and Stock is second to none. K. C. Hanson and Chris Spinks have done a cracking good job of getting this series going and were supportive of the project from the beginning. K. C. has a wealth of experience in commentary production and he gave me some golden advice as a new editor. Third, I have to thank my family as always, including my wife Naomi and my daughters Alexis and Alyssa. Fourth, several people read and offered helpful comments on an earlier draft, including Lynn Cohick, Sean Du Toit, and Ian Smith, and I am most grateful for their remarks. Fifth, I would like to dedicate this book to my good friend Ben Myers, who is making theology in the antipodes fashionable again and is my *syndoulos* in the kingdom of Christ. His dedication to the theological craft is inspiring. May his tribe increase!

---

1. Unfortunately the commentaries on Colossians by Jerry L. Sumney and Douglas J. Moo came out too late for me to be able to make use of them.

Abbreviations

AB	Anchor Bible
ABRL	Anchor Bible Reference Library
ACCS	Ancient Christian Commentary on Scripture
BDAG	Walter Bauer, F. W. Danker, W. F. Arndt, and F. W. Gingrich, *A Greek-English Lexicon of the New Testament and Other Early Christian Literature*. 3rd ed.; Chicago: University of Chicago Press, 2000
BDF	F. Blass, A. Debrunner, and R. W. Funk, editors, *A Greek Grammar of the New Testament and Other Early Christian Literature* (9th ed.; Chicago: University of Chicago Press, 1961)
Bib	*Biblica*
BSac	*Bibliotheca Sacra*
BST	Bible Speaks Today
CGTC	Cambridge Greek Testament Commentary
ECC	Eerdmans Critical Commentary
EDNT	H. Balz and G. Schneider, editors, *Exegetical Dictionary of the New Testament*. 3 vols.; Grand Rapids: Eerdmans, 1990
EvQ	*Evangelical Quarterly*
ESCJ	Études sur le christianisme et le judaïsme (Studies in Christianity and Judaism)
ESV	English Standard Version
ExpTim	*Expository Times*
FRLANT	Forschungen zur Religion und Literatur des Alten und Neuen Testaments
HTR	*Harvard Theological Review*
ICC	International Critical Commentary
IVPNTC	InterVarsity Press New Testament Commentary
JBL	*Journal of Biblical Literature*
JETS	*Journal of the Evangelical Theological Society*
JSNT	*Journal for the Study of the New Testament*
JSNTSup	JSNT Supplement Series
JTS	*Journal of Theological Studies*
KJV	King James Version

LightAE	Adolf Deissman, *Light from the Ancient East.* Translated by L. R. M. Strachan. Peabody, MA: Hendrickson, 1995
LCL	Loeb Classical Library
LNTS	Library of New Testament Studies
LXX	Septuagint
MNTC	Moffatt New Testament Commentary
NASB	New American Standard Bible
NCB	New Century Bible
NDIEC	G. H. R. Horsley and S. R. Llewelyn, editors, *New Documents Illustrating Early Christianity.* 9 vols. Grand Rapids: Eerdmans, 1976–87
NEB	New English Bible
NeoT	*Neotestamentica*
NET	New English Translation
NIB	New Interpreter's Bible
NIGTC	New International Greek Testament Commentary
NIV	New International Version
NIVAC	NIV Application Commentary
NJB	New Jerusalem Bible
NLT	New Living Translation
NovTSup	Supplements to Novum Testamentum
NPNF	*Nicene and Post-Nicene Fathers*
NRSV	New Revised Standard Version
NTC	New Testament Commentary
NTG	New Testament Guides
NTM	New Testament Monographs
NTS	*New Testament Studies*
ÖTKNT	Ökumenischer Taschenbuch-Kommentar zum Neuen Testament
OTP	James H. Charlesworth, editor, *Old Testament Pseudepigrapha.* 2 vols. ABRL. New York: Doubleday, 1983, 1985
PC	Proclamation Commentaries
PSt	Pauline Studies
RevExp	*Review and Expositor*
REB	Revised English Bible
RGG	K. Galling and H. von Campenhausen, editors. *Religion in Geschichte und Gegenwart.* 3rd ed. 7 vols. Tübingen: Mohr/Siebeck, 1957–65
RSV	Revised Standard Version
SBLMS	Society of Biblical Literature Monograph Series
SBT	Studies in Biblical Theology

SP	Sacra pagina
SUNT	Studien zur Umwelt des Neuen Testaments
TEV	Today's English Version
TDNT	G. Kittel and G. Friedrich, editors, *Theological Dictionary of the New Testament*. Translated by G. W. Bromiley. 10 vols. Grand Rapids: Eerdmans, 1964–1976
TH	Two Horizons
TNIV	Today's New International Version
TNTC	Tyndale New Testament Commentaries
TSAJ	Texte und Studium zum antiken Judentum
TynBul	*Tyndale Bulletin*
WUNT	Wissenschaftliche Untersuchungen zum Neuen Testament
ZNW	*Zeitschrift für die neutestamentliche Wissenschaft und die Kunde der älteren Kirche*

Ancient Sources

1QH	Thanksgiving Hymns
1QM	War Scroll
1QS	Rule of the Community
4Q186	Zodiacal Physiognomy
4Q400–5	Songs of the Sabbath Sacrifice
4Q510	Songs of the Sage
4Q534	Elect of God
Apoc. Ab.	*Apocalypse of Abraham*
Apoc. Paul	*Apocalypse of Paul*
Apoc. Zeph.	*Apocalypse of Zephaniah*
Ascen. Isa.	*Martyrdom and Ascension of Isaiah* 6–11
Augustine *Civ.*	*De civitate Dei* (*The City of God*)
Babylonian Talmud (*b.*)	
Menah.	*Menahot*
Sanh.	*Sanhedrin*
Bar	Baruch
2 Bar.	*2 Baruch* (*Syriac Apocalypse*)
Barn.	*Barnabas*

Calpurnius Siculus
    Ecl.   *Eclogues*

CD   Cairo Genizah copy of the *Damascus Document*

Cicero
    Flac.   *Pro Flacco*

1 Clem.   *1 Clement*

Did.   *Didache*

Dionysius of Halicarnassus
    Ant. rom.   *Antiquitates romanae* (*Roman History*)

1 En.   *1 Enoch* (*Ethiopic Apocalypse*)

2 En.   *2 Enoch* (*Slavonic Apocalypse*)

3 En.   *3 Enoch* (*Hebrew Apocalypse*)

Epictetus
    Disc.   *Discourses*

Ep. Arist.   *Epistle of Aristeas*

Eusebius
    Chron.   *Chronicon* (*Chronicle*)

Gos. Thom.   *Gospel of Thomas*

Gk. Apoc. Ezra   *Greek Apocalypse of Ezra*

Hippolytus
    Haer.   *Refutatio omnium haeresium*
                  (*Refutation of All Heresies*)

Jdt   Judith

John Chrysostom
    Hom. Col.   *Homiliae in epistulum ad Colossesnses*

Jos. Asen.   *Joseph and Aseneth*

Josephus
    Ag. Ap.   *Against Apion*
    Ant.   *Jewish Antiquities*
    J. W.   *Jewish Wars*

Jub.   *Jubilees*

Justin
    Dial. Tryph.   *Dialogue with Trypho*

Juvenal
  Sat.   *Satirae* (*Satires*)

Livy
  Hist.   *History of Rome*

1–4 Macc   1–4 Maccabees

Mishnah (*m.*)
  ʿ*Abod. Zar.*   ʿ*Abodah Zarah*
  Ber.   *Berakhot*

Odes Sol.   *Odes of Solomon*

Origen
  Cels.   *Contra Celsum* (*Against Celsus*)

Philo
  Conf.   *De confusione linguarum* (*On the Confusion of Tongues*)
  Decal.   *De decalogo* (*On the Decalogue*)
  Det.   *Quod deterius potiori insidiari soleat* (*That the Worse Attacks*
                    the Better)
  Flacc.   *In Flaccum* (*Against Flaccum*)
  Fug.   *De fuga et inventione* (*On Flight and Finding*)
  Gig.   *De gigantibus* (*On Giants*)
  Hypoth.   *Hypothetica*
  Leg.   *Legum allegoriae* (*Allegorical Interpretation*)
  Legat.   *Legatio ad Gaium* (*On the Embassy to Gaius*)
  Migr.   *De migratione Abrahami* (*On the Migration of Abraham*)
  Mos.   *De vita Mosis* (*On the Life of Moses*)
  Opif.   *De opifico mundi* (*On the Creation of the World*)
  Plant.   *De plantatione* (*On Planting*)
  Prob.   *Quod omnis probus liber sit* (*That Every Good Person*
                    Is Free)
  QE   *Quaestiones et solutions in Exodum* (*Questions and Answers*
                    on Exodus)
  Sacr.   *De sacrificiis Abelis et Caini* (*On the Sacrifices of Cain and Abel*)
  Somn.   *De somnis* (*On Dreams*)
  Spec.   *De specialibus legibus* (*On the Special Laws*)

Philostratus
  Vit. Apoll.   *Vita Apollonii*

Plato
  Tim.   *Timaeus*

Pliny the Younger
    Ep.   *Epistolae*

Pss. Sol.   *Psalms of Solomon*

Sir   Sirach

Seneca
    Ep.   *Epistulae morales*

Strabo
    Geogr.   *Geographica (Geography)*

T. Ab.   *Testament of Abraham*

T. Isaac   *Testament of Isaac*

T. Job   *Testament of Job*

T. Levi   *Testament of Levi*

Tacitus
    Agr.   *Agricola*
    Hist.   *Historiae*

Tertullian
    Jejun.   *De jujunio adversus psychicos (On Fasting, against the Psychics)*

Tob   Tobit

Wis   Wisdom

Xenophon
    Anab.   *Anabasis*

Introduction to Colossians and Philemon

> When I open the chapel doors of the Epistle to the Colossians it is as if Johann Sebastian himself sat at the organ.[1]

> The singular loftiness of the mind of Paul, though it may be seen to greater advantage in his other writings which treat of weightier matters, is also attested by this Epistle [to Philemon], in which, while he handles a subject otherwise low and mean, he rises to God with his wonted elevation. Sending back a runaway slave and thief, he supplicates pardon for him. But in pleading this cause, he discourses about Christian forbearance with such ability, that he appears to speak about the interests of the whole Church rather than the private affairs of a single individual. On behalf of a man of the lowest condition, he demeans himself so modestly and humbly, that nowhere else is the meekness of his temper painted in a more lively manner.[2]

CITY OF COLOSSAE

Colossae was a city in the Lycus Valley located within southwestern Phrygia in the interior of Asia Minor. Colossae was once a densely populated and wealthy city according to Xenophon, a city through which Xerxes and his army passed in 480 BCE.[3] The Greek geographer Strabo described Colossae in his time as a *polisma*, or small city.[4] In 133 BCE the last king of Pergamum bequeathed his kingdom to the Romans who later reorganized it as the province of Asia. The Lycus Valley was eventually incorporated into the Roman Empire and remained so for many centuries. By Paul's time Colossae was dwarfed by the larger cities of Hierapolis and Laodicea also in the Lycus Valley.

1. Deissman 1957: 107.
2. Calvin 1979a: 348.
3. Xenophon *Anab.* 1.2.6.
4. Strabo *Geogr.* 12.8.13.

There was a sizable Jewish population in the Lycus Valley. Seleucus Nicator (ca. 358–281 BCE), the founder of the Seleucid kingdom encompassing Asia Minor, granted civic rights to the Jews in all the cities that he founded and Antiochus II (ca. 286–46 BCE) planted Jewish colonists in the cities of Ionia.[5] Antiochus III (ca. 241–187 BCE) settled some two thousand Jewish families from Babylon and Mesopotamia in the regions of Lydia and Phrygia, and Philo refers to the large population of Jews in every city of Asia Minor.[6] Laodicea in particular was a collection point for payment of the temple tax by Jews living in the region, and in 62 BCE the proconsul of Asia Lucius Valerius Flaccus attempted to seize the collection, which, according to Cicero, consisted of twenty pounds of gold.[7] If the temple tax was a half shekel or two drachmae, that could represent a collection from Jewish males numbering as many as ten thousand, though a slightly lower figure might be more cautious.[8] Like other Anatolian cities, Colossae probably had a substantial Jewish population (possibly between one and two thousand persons) and at least one synagogue or prayer house. A number of Jewish sarcophagi in Hierapolis have been collected together by Walter Ameling, indicating a sizable Jewish presence in the Lycus Valley.[9] Hierapolis and Laodicea suffered extensive damage from an earthquake that shook the region in the early 60s CE and we can safely assume that Colossae suffered the same fate. Laodicea was rebuilt using funds from within the city, but we do not know what happened to Colossae or if it survived the earthquake or not.[10] There is no evidence of habitation in Colossae after 63–64 CE until coins reappear in the late second century.[11]

Colossae has never been excavated; however, excavations are planned in a joint project directed by Flinders University (Australia) and Pamukkale University (Turkey).[12] We can anxiously await the results since

5. Josephus *Ant.* 12.119, 125.

6. Ibid. 12.147–53; Philo *Legat.* 245.

7. Cicero *Flac.* 28.68.

8. Cf. Bruce 1984a: 5; Trebilco 1991: 13–14.

9. Ameling 2004: 398–440.

10. Tacitus *Annals* 14.27; and according to Eusebius (*Chron.* 1.21) all three major towns in the Lycus Valley were destroyed. Strabo (*Geogr.* 12.8.16) wrote that the entire region was known as a centre of repeated catastrophes.

11. Lincoln 2000: 580.

12. See "Colossae," online: http://ehlt.flinders.edu.au/theology/institute/colossae/.

it may significantly alter much of what we claim to know about Judaism, indigenous religions, and Christianity in Colossae. In fact, Colossians commentaries may need to be rewritten in light of the evidence that emerges.

RELATIONSHIP OF COLOSSIANS TO EPHESIANS

Colossians stands conceptually between Galatians and Ephesians, while Philemon is probably the closest in style to Philippians. Colossians has a mix of Pauline polemics indicative of Galatians and the lavish language and high Christology of Ephesians. Ephesians and Colossians are similar in many respects as both are said to be delivered by Tychicus (Col 4:7–9; Eph 6:21), they exhibit similar language, theological concerns (e.g., "mystery," "raised with Christ," catholic "Church"), and share fifteen words not found elsewhere in other New Testament writings. The literary parallels between Colossians and Ephesians are numerous (see the table below) and have usually led to a literary relationship being posited between the two documents.[13] Although some have argued that Colossians depends on Ephesians, the reverse seems far more likely given the use of Old Testament quotations and allusions in Ephesians that is lacking in Colossians. These quotations and allusions are more likely to have been added than subtracted by an author or redactor. There is also a greater focus on the church universal and more attention given to the Holy Spirit in Ephesians, which suggests theological explication of something found in Colossians. These letters are genetically related, but also somewhat independent of one another given the differences in purpose, audience, and even contents, showing how complicated the issue of literary dependency really is.[14] The historical circumstances of their common relationship can only be judged once the questions of the authorship and the provenance of Colossians and Philemon are satisfactorily answered.

13. See the synoptic parallels provided by Kooten 2003 and further lists of parallels in Talbert 2007: 4–5. I find that a comparison of Eph 6:21–22 and Col 4:7–8 clearly supports some sort of literary relationship between the two writings. Yet F. C. Baur overstates the case when he writes, "The whole contents of the two Epistles are substantially the same," and asserts that Ephesians and Colossians are so interwoven "that they stand or fall together in their claim to apostolic origin" ([1873–75] 2003: vol. 2, 4, 44).

14. On the independent nature of Colossians from Ephesians, see Ellis 1999: 110–11; and Talbert 2007: 4–6; while Barth and Blanke (1994: 72–114) argue that the problem of literary dependency is unsolved and perhaps unsolvable.

Ephesians	Colossians	Section
1:1–2	1:1–2	authors and addressees
1:22–23	1:17–19	headship of the Messiah
2:13–18	1:20–22	reconciliation through the cross
4:16	2:19	unity in the body
5:19–20	3:16	Christian worship
5:22–6:9	3:18–4:1	household code
6:19–20	4:3	Paul's evangelism activities
6:21–22	4:7–8	Tychicus's commendation

AUTHORSHIP

Philemon is ordinarily regarded as genuinely Pauline and no new reasons have been adduced to doubt this fact. The style and vocabulary of Philemon, typified by the opening and closing sections, is characteristically Pauline. The overall linguistic variation of the contents also remains well within the diversity attested by the undisputed letters of Paul. Philemon would also seem to be an odd letter for a pseudepigrapher to compose given that it lacks doctrinally polemical content. Thus, we possess every confidence that it was written by Paul. The authorship of Colossians, on the other hand, is (with Second Thessalonians, Ephesians, and the Pastoral Epistles) disputed.[15] It is proposed by many that Colossians is a pseudonymous letter (but not necessarily an ill-intended forgery) written in Paul's name by a post-Pauline disciple. It was given the appearance of verisimilitude by fictitiously addressing the letter to an obscure community that Paul did not visit and one that probably ceased to exist after the earthquake of 61–62 CE. This would ensure the unlikelihood of any one being able to falsify its origins, whereas it was really intended as a general admonition for churches in Roman Asia sometime around the 70–80s.[16]

15. Technically, Ephesians and the Pastoral Epistles are the so-called "Deutero-Pauline" letters, while Colossians and Second Thessalonians are the proper "Disputed Pauline" letters. Cf. Mead 1986: 118.

16. Cf. recently Lohse 1971: 181; Pokorný 1991: 21; Lincoln 2000: 580; Wilson 2005: 17–19; but against this scenario is Schweizer 1982: 19–21; Wedderburn 1987: 70; Dunn 1996: 37.

There are a number of legitimate reasons for disputing the letter's authenticity: (1) The language of Colossians is somewhat different from the *Hauptbriefe* or "main letters" of Paul—Romans, 1–2 Corinthians, and Galatians—as well as the undisputed letters of First Thessalonians, Philippians, and Philemon. (2) The theology of Colossians is also said to be more developed than the main epistles, particularly in its high Christology, catholic ecclesiology, and realized eschatology. Nonetheless, most acknowledge that Colossians still has a very Pauline buzz about it in terms of cadence, ethos, tone, and content; it is as close to his mind as one might expect. For this reason, many commentators have followed Ernst Käsemann's dictum: "if genuine, as late as possible, because of the content and style; if not genuine, as early as conceivable."[17]

It is my contention, however, that despite some valid objections, Colossians is authentic and written during the apostle's own lifetime in collaboration with his coworkers.[18] First of all, a number of authors have argued that Colossians is pseudonymous based on statistical and linguistic comparisons with the undisputed letters.[19] For instance, there are thirty-four *hapax legomena* in Colossians (i.e., words that occur nowhere else in the New Testament), twenty-eight words that appear elsewhere in the New Testament but nowhere else in Paul, several stylistic peculiarities such as synonymous expressions (e.g., "praying and asking," 1:9) and dependent genitives (e.g., "the word of truth, of the gospel," 1:5), and the absence of key Pauline words like "law," "righteousness/justification," "salvation" and "sin" that one might expect Paul to have used in tackling a philosophy with Jewish traits.[20] Yet the linguistic data may not be fully decisive against Pauline authorship.

(1) We do not have a pure "control" sample of Paul's own writings that we can be absolutely sure are exclusively his own wording/writing and thus make use of it as a template for comparison with Colossians.

17. Käsemann, *RGG* 3:728.

18. Cf. especially the positive case for Pauline authorship in O'Brien 1982: xli–xlix; Smith 2006: 6–14. In particular, it seems hard to place Col 4:7–17 in a post-Pauline context. Furthermore, deSilva (2004: 701) argues that the contents are exactly what we would expect from an astute pastoral leader concerning: (a) reliance on shared traditions, (b) Paul's brief reflection on his own calling in God's purpose, and (c) personal matters like prayer requests, personal greetings, and personal exhortations.

19. Cf. Bujard 1973; Kiley 1986; Collins 2005.

20. Cf. the data listed in Lohse 1971: 84–88; McL. Wilson 2005: 12–13.

Apart from the fact of textual variations in the manuscript tradition itself, we have to admit that even the undisputed letters of Paul may be the result of an amanuensis or secretary and are not necessarily from Paul's own hand. So comparing the style and language of Romans and Colossians may not in actual fact be comparing an authentic and pseudonymous piece of writing, but amount to comparing Tertius (Rom 16:22) and Timothy (Col 1:1) as Paul's secretary and coauthor in two different letters. We would do well also to consider the observation of Matthew Brook O'Donnell about the limits of statistical analysis:

> It seems unlikely that by simply counting words it is possible to differentiate between authors. While a particular author may have a core or base vocabulary, as well as an affinity for certain words (or combination/collocation of words), there are many factors, for instance, age, further education, social setting, rhetorical purpose and so on, that restrict or expand this core set of lexical items. In spite of this, New Testament attribution studies and many commentaries (sadly, some rather recent ones at that) have placed considerable weight on counting the number of words found in one letter but not found in a group of letters assumed to be authentic.[21]

(2) It should be noted that a significant number of *hapax* also occur in Galatians, Philippians, and even Philemon. As for absences of key terminology, the term "justify" does not appear at all in First Thessalonians or Philippians, while "law" is absent from Second Corinthians, and even "salvation" does not appear in Galatians or First Corinthians.[22] In addition, there are some genuine stylistic and grammatical affinities with Paul's other letters in Colossians which are evident in the opening greeting, thanksgiving section, epistle closing, plus the presence of typical Pauline expressions throughout Colossians (e.g., "in Messiah"). We also find conceptual similarities in terms of letter structure and theological content (e.g., freedom from Jewish practices).[23]

(3) There are cogent reasons why the language of Colossians is different to the other Pauline letters, such as the fact that Paul seems to be cit-

---

21. O'Donnell 2005: 388.
22. Lohse 1971: 87; O'Brien 1982: xliii.
23. Lohse 1971: 84–85, 87, 182–83; McL. Wilson 2005: 14.

ing a lot of early traditional Christian material (Col 1:12–20; 3:5–14; 3:18–4:1; and perhaps 2:9–15)[24] and mirroring some of the language of the philosophy that had become controversial in Colossae (e.g., Col 1:19; 2:9, 18). From a rhetorical vantage point, the letters to Ephesus and Colossae, cities in Roman Asia, may deliberately contain an Asiatic rhetoric that was often more flowery, ornamented, poetic, and slightly pompous compared to its Greek counterpart, thus accounting for the more descriptive and expansive nature of the language.[25] Rhetorical training itself urged the necessity of adapting one's style, language, and content to fit the occasion depending on the persona needed for the speaker or author.[26]

(4)   Colossians does not properly fit the genre of a pseudepigraphal letter, which is ordinarily attributed to a famous figure of the past to one of his contemporaries and is intended to be of interest to its real readers only in a general sense. The problem in Colossae seems to be quite specific and there is no attempt to bridge the divide between fictive readers and real readers by means of a "testament" or other literary device.[27] Ultimately, there is nothing about the language, style, and form that is wildly anachronistic or cannot be plausibly placed within the context of Paul's own lifetime, and much of the structure and language sounds evidently genuine.

Second, regarding the theology of Colossians, Lohse claims that the thought of Colossians exhibits Pauline features but is an example of a Pauline theology that has undergone a profound change in many respects.[28] To begin with, on ecclesiology, in the undisputed letters the "church" is always the church local (e.g., Gal 1:2; 1 Thess 1:1; 1 Cor 1:2; 2

---

24. Cf. Cannon (1983: 49): "Based on the United Bible Societies' text of Colossians, of the 114 lines of text in the first two chapters, thirty-four (or thirty percent) of them are drawn from traditional material and twenty-five of them are careful applications of the traditional material. This means that over fifty percent of the first two chapters of Colossians are influenced by words, ideas, and modes of expression that were already existing in the early church. Any judgment made about the authorship of the letter must keep this important factor fully in mind."

25. Cf. Reicke 2001: 75; Bird 2008b, 377–78.

26. Witherington 2007: 1–2, esp. the quote from L. T. Johnson in n. 2.

27. Cf. Bauckham 1988: 492.

28. Lohse 1971: 180 (see all of 177–83); cf. Baur 2003 [1873–75]: vol. 2, 7–8, 35–38 on the apparently developed Christology of Colossians.

Cor 1:2) whereas in Colossians (and Ephesians) the *ekklēsia* is both the "church" local (Col 1:2; 4:15–16; cf. Eph 1:1) and the "Church" universal (Col 1:18, 24; cf. Eph 1:22; 3:10, 21; 5:23–25, 27, 29, 32).[29] Still, Paul viewed the churches as a pan-Roman Empire movement who were in close association with one another; there is nothing inconceivable about him referring to "Church" in this more trans-local sense. Concerning baptism and eschatology, Colossians refers to the baptized as those not only buried with Christ but risen with him as well (2:11–12; 3:1; cf. Eph 2:5–6), whereas in Romans the resurrection of Christians is still future (Rom 6:4–5). Yet in Romans, Paul can also refer to believers having been "glorified" in the past tense (Rom 8:30) and glory also relates to a present experience of the new covenant (2 Cor 3:18), which is not too many steps away from Col 2:11–13; 3:1. What is more, Col 2:11–12 is not saying that the resurrection has already taken place (as attributed to Hymenaeus and Philetus in 2 Tim 2:17–18), but as Todd Still notes it merely employs resurrection language to speak of a "believer's conversion to, union with, and transformation through Christ." A future resurrection of believers is implied by 1:18 where Jesus is the "firstborn from among the dead," which suggests that Christians will follow in his train (see 1 Cor 15:20).[30] Even with a strong emphasis on realized eschatology in several places (1:12–13; 2:11–12, 15, 20; 3:1), the future horizon has not disappeared completely in Colossians (1:5, 22, 24, 27–28; 3:4, 6, 10, 24–25) and it retains a reasonable amount of congruity with the undisputed Pauline letters.[31] Likewise, the Christology of 1:15–20 and 2:9–10 may sound grandiose, yet it is not out of order with 1 Cor 8:4–6; 2 Cor 8:9; and Phil 2:5–11, which contain traditional material as well. The motif of victory in 2:15 is analogous to 1 Cor 15:54–57 and Rom 8:29–39, 16:20 too. Similarly, the household code of 3:18—4:1 is not the sexist regulations of a Pauline disciple who did not share the apostle's egalitarian view of women, but stands as part of a natural trajectory from other elements of Paul's letters about women and households (e.g., 1 Cor 7:1–40; 11:3–16; 14:33–35). In sum, the question of how much difference and development it takes to illegitimate Pauline authorship is unquantifiable and is therefore grossly subjective. What a

29. I am unpersuaded by O'Brien (1982: xlv–xlvi, 57–61) who understands the "church" in 1:18 as a reference to heavenly assembly around the risen Christ.

30. Still 2004: 133.

31. Cf. Sappington 1991: 226; Gorman 2004: 477; Still 2004: 130–35; deSilva 2004: 697–98.

later disciple of Paul theologically inferred from Paul's writings fifteen years after his death might not be any different to what Paul and his co-workers inferred themselves while writing to believers from a position of captivity that naturally gave over to exercises of reflection.

There is of course no getting away from the valid perception that Colossians does sound a little different from, say, Galatians and First Thessalonians in language. Colossians develops motifs which, though genuinely Pauline, are emphasized and explored in new ways. What are we to make of this then? James Dunn regards Colossians as a "bridge" between the Pauline and post-Pauline periods and contends that it was composed at the end of Paul's lifetime, but by somebody other than Paul at Paul's own behest and approval, hence the autograph.[32] The plausibility of this scenario is enhanced by the observation of Margaret MacDonald: "If we think of the authorship of Pauline works as a communal enterprise undertaken by Paul and his entourage, the sharp distinction between authentic and unauthentic epistles is significantly reduced."[33] I would add that this does not make Paul merely the authorizer rather than the author! He may have had varying degrees of input into his various letters ranging from writing them himself (Philemon), writing them with a coauthor (Colossians), dictating them (Romans), or authorizing their composition based on an earlier piece of correspondence (Ephesians). Given those qualifications, I have no hesitation in affirming Colossians as authentically Pauline and written in association with others such as Tychicus, Epaphras, Onesimus, Luke, and especially Timothy.[34]

PROVENANCE OF COLOSSIANS AND PHILEMON

Given the qualified assumption of Pauline authorship of Philemon, Colossians, and (more loosely) Ephesians, when and where were the former two epistles written? What we can say is that Colossians and Philemon were probably written in relatively close temporal proximity to each other because the five same persons are mentioned in Paul's greetings in both

---

32. Dunn 1996: 38–39.

33. MacDonald 2008: 44.

34. On Timothy as author see Schweizer 1982: 23–25; Dunn 1996: 38–39. It is interesting that two manuscripts state that Colossians was written "from Rome through Tychicus and Onesimus" (075, 1739, 1881, and several Byzantine witnesses), which associates these Pauline coworkers with the letter's composition and delivery.

letters, namely, Luke, Mark, Demas, Aristarchus, and Epaphras (Col 4:10–14; Phlm 23–24). Timothy is named as coauthor in both letters (Col 1:1; Phlm 1), a sending of Onesimus is referred to in both letters (Col 4:9; Phlm 10, 12, 17), Archippus is mentioned in both (Col 4:17; Phlm 2), and the two letters are undersigned with Paul's own hand (Col 4:18; Phlm 19). One peculiar fact is that Colossians makes no reference to any potential conflict between Onesimus and Philemon, which one might expect on the return of a runaway slave to his owner which could adversely affect relations within the community (see Paul's exhortation for unity and reconciliation among Euodia and Syntyche in Phil 4:2). Rather, in Col 4:9 Onesimus is also regarded as a faithful and experienced coworker. The letter to Philemon does not mention Tychicus. It would seem that there was a gap between the composition of Philemon and Colossians,[35] in which case the sending back of Onesimus in Phlm 12 and the sending of Onesimus with Tychicus in Col 4:9 may reflect two different journeys of Onesimus to Colossae separated by several months or even up to a year. I surmise that Paul first sent Onesimus back to Philemon. Philemon was reconciled to Onesimus and subsequently returned Onesimus to Paul's service as requested by Paul. Sometime later, the news of an encounter with a certain "philosophy" in Colossae was relayed to Paul and his coworkers who responded by writing Colossians and sending Tychicus and Onesimus to deliver the letter to Colossae and a circular letter (Ephesians) to the other churches of Asia and principally to Laodicea. I find this scenario plausible, though admittedly unverifiable.

So where was Paul when this happened? He was obviously in captivity (Phlm 1, 10, 23; Col 4:3, 10, 18), but which period of captivity, since he refers to imprisonments in the plural in 2 Cor 11:23 (cf. *1 Clem.* 5.6)? The main candidates are Ephesus (ca. 55–57 CE) or Rome (ca. 61–66 CE).[36] This subject is one of the most perplexing facing students of Colossians. The problem is mirrored in text-critical observations since some manuscripts (e.g., A and B) regard Colossians as written from

---

35. Cf. Gnilka 1982: 5; Schweizer 1982: 24–25; Pokorný 1991: 9.

36. Another option put forward (e.g., Ellis 1999: 266–75; Reicke 2001: 75) is Caesarea (Acts 23:33—26:32) where, according to Acts, Paul was imprisoned for two years (Acts 24:27). But Paul had no hope for an early release which is reflected in Philemon (v. 22). Caesarea would not have provided a likely outlet for Paul's evangelistic work referred to in Colossians (Col 4:3–4). Caesarea is also a less likely refuge for a runaway slave (see Martin 1973: 24).

Rome. Yet the Marcionite prologue declares it written from Ephesus. To add further complications the Marcionite prologue places the composition of Philemon and Ephesians in Rome. Even if we take into account the movements of Paul's coworkers according to the Pauline letters and Acts, the evidence still remains ambiguous.[37] The internal evidence of Colossians and Philemon themselves are not decisive, nor does taking into account the wider New Testament provide us with a clear cut answer. Instead, we have to weigh the arguments for and against an Ephesian or Roman setting.[38]

Roman Setting: Pro and Con. In favor of a Roman provenance is that we know Paul did experience a prolonged period of imprisonment in Rome, which is attested by Acts (Acts 28:16) and other early Christian literature.[39] The letter to the Philippians was also written from captivity and many think it sent from Rome (Phil 1:13–14). Unfortunately, there is no clear reference to a Roman imprisonment in the undisputed letters of Paul, which is no small fact, and must be taken into consideration. Second, in Phlm 9 Paul calls himself an "old man," which suggests that it was written at the end of his life. However, this might be a phrase used rhetorically to get Philemon to respect *his* elder and *the* apostle. Third, and perhaps the strongest argument for a Roman provenance, is that the theology of Colossians seems to represent a maturation and development

---

37. (1) Timothy can be placed in Ephesus (Acts 19:22; 1 Cor 16:10; 1 Tim 1:3) but not Rome (unless Phil 1:1 was written from Rome). (2) Tychicus is linked to Rome and Ephesus (2 Tim 4:12) but towards the end of Paul's imprisonment. (3) Aristarchus was apparently in Ephesus during the riot there (Acts 19:29) and he probably sailed onto Rome with Paul (Acts 27:2). (4) Demas is only linked with Paul in his final imprisonment and noted for his desertion (2 Tim 4:10). (5) If Luke was Paul's travelling companion after Troas (Acts 16:11) he may have been with Paul in Ephesus and probably accompanied him to Rome, hence "we came to Rome" (Acts 28:14, 16; cf. 2 Tim 4:11). (6) John Mark had broken off from Paul (Acts 15:37–41) during an earlier missionary journey so the reference to him with Paul in Col 4:10 and Phlm 24 is all the more peculiar. It means that reconciliation has probably occurred. He is placed in Rome by 1 Pet 5:13 and in Ephesus by 2 Tim 4:11.

38. For a Roman setting see, e.g., Kümmel 1975: 347–48; O'Brien 1982: xlix–liv; Dunn 1996: 41; Gorman 2004: 478; Witherington 2007: 22–24; and for an Ephesian setting, e.g., Lohse 1971: 166–67 (for Philemon); Martin 1973: 30; Schweizer 1982: 25–26; Wright 1986: 34–39; Stuckenbruck 2003: 127; deSilva 2004: 668 (for Philemon).

39. The Pastoral Epistles (if authentic) also testify to a second Roman imprisonment (2 Tim 1:17), but Colossians could not have been written during a second Roman imprisonment since Timothy was in Ephesus at this time and unable to be cosender of the letter to the Colossians.

of Pauline thought. This is attributable no doubt to Paul's own theological reflection on Christology and ecclesiology, but also to the interpretation of Paul's thought that began with his coworkers like Timothy and had already started to weave its way into the letter. Still, this does not necessitate a later date after Paul's death, since Paul's theology clearly developed somewhat during the short time span between Galatians (ca. 49 CE) and Romans (ca. 55–56 CE). We do not know how much of the so-called developed theology of Colossians is attributable to the interpretive insights of Paul's coworkers and their inferences about Paul's theology, which could have been made from any location or residence with time for writing and reflection. Fourth, Rome would be a very good place for a runaway slave to hide in the massive population of the city, yet it was also a long way to travel (approximately 1200 miles by sea) when other cities in Asia Minor and Syria such as Ephesus and Antioch were nearer and large enough to afford a veil of protection. Fifth, a Roman setting was the preferred view of patristic authors, but it was not unanimous, and constitutes tertiary evidence at best.

Ephesian Setting: Pro and Con. The case for an Ephesian setting is strengthened by accounts that place Paul there more than once (1 Cor 16:8; Acts 18:19–21 and esp. 19:1–20:1) and for three years during his Aegean mission (Acts 19:8–10). That Paul experienced imprisonment in Ephesus is arguably implied in 2 Cor 1:8 where the apostle refers to the hardships experienced by him and his companions in Asia, and also in 1 Cor 15:32 where Paul speaks metaphorically of fighting wild beasts in Ephesus.[40] However, there is no clear evidence for an Ephesian imprisonment in Paul's letters or in Acts. Second, it can be argued that Ephesus and Colossae, only one hundred miles apart, make far more plausible the flight of Onesimus, the delegation of Tychicus/Onesimus, any travels back and forth by Epaphras, the forthcoming visit of John Mark, and the possible visit of Paul to Philemon. This flurry of comings and goings is more likely than a series of lengthy sea journeys that were dangerous and took weeks or months at a time. Third, Paul's request in Phlm 22 that a guest room be prepared for him is more realistic given an Ephesian imprisonment. If it was Paul's plan to go further west after his release from confinement in Rome, then a journey to Colossae to visit Philemon would have meant

40. A number of Pauline chronologists (e.g., Knox 1950: 71; Jewett 1979: 103; Lüdemann 1984: 263; Riesner 1998: 213–16) either support or allow the possibility of an Ephesian imprisonment.

significantly revising (or reversing) that plan. Alternatively, the remark may simply be rhetorical and a polite wish to visit but with no actual intent to do so (my in-laws in Australia threaten to visit me in Scotland all the time but thankfully only rarely do so) and remain consistent with a Roman setting. Fourth, according to ancient sources there was an earthquake that destroyed parts of the Lycus Valley, especially Laodicea, ca. 61–62 CE.[41] We do not hear of any references to Christians there in extant sources and only Laodicea is mentioned among the seven churches that John the Seer wrote to at the end of the first century (Rev 1:11; 3:14). Even so, we do not know for sure how the Christians in Colossae were affected by the earthquake and what impact it had upon their lives. True enough, Paul does not mention the earthquake when we might expect him to do so, but neither does he mention other "seismic" events such as the expulsion of Jews from Rome under Claudius (49 CE) and their return under Nero (54 CE) when he wrote to the Romans.

The evidence is tightly balanced (and I confess to having changed my mind a number of times). The answer, I think, lies not with internal evidence from Colossians or Philemon, but with the letter to the Philippians and the movements of Timothy. He is named as cosender of Colossians and Philemon (Col 1:1; Phlm 1). To that we can add the observations that Timothy is also named as cosender of Philippians (Phil 1:1), Philippians is also written from captivity (Phil 1:13–14), and Philippians is similar to Philemon in at least two other respects: both look forward to Paul's eventual release from prison (Phlm 22; Phil 1:19–26; 2:24), and there are several stylistic similarities between them as noted by Francis Watson.[42] By way of deduction, my line of reasoning runs Timothy → Philippians → Philemon → Colossians → Location! Thus, the circumstances of Philippians and Timothy are crucial for the provenance and date of Colossians/Philemon.

Philippians could have been written from either Rome or Ephesus, but the internal and external evidence to decide the matter is much stronger. There is a reference to the "praetorian guard" in Phil 1:13, which may denote the elite body guard unit of the emperor in Rome, which also functioned as a police force in the capital. There is also a reference to a greeting from those of "Caesar's household" in Phil 4:22, which would naturally fit a Roman setting. However, "praetorian" can mean more

41. Tacitus *Annals* 14.27.

42. Watson 2007: 141–42.

generally "palace guard" or "military headquarters" (Matt 27:27; Mark 15:16; John 18:28, 33; 19:9; Acts 23:35). And "Caesar's household" might denote the imperial staff stationed at an imperial residence in Ephesus since this was also the Roman capital of western Asia. Given the rancorous language in Philippians, debates with Paul's opponents in Galatia and Corinth still seem very recent (e.g., Phil 3:2–11, 18–19). It is also unlikely that Roman prisoners would be incarcerated in the emperor's own residence. Furthermore, there is no reference to Timothy accompanying Paul to Rome in Acts 28, but he is placed in Ephesus during Paul's extended ministry there (1 Cor 16:8–10). We also know from Acts that Timothy engaged in one or more trips to Greece and Macedonia from Ephesus (Acts 19:22). Thus, Paul's intent to send Timothy to Philippi (Phil 2:19) is more likely to comport with his travels to Greece and Macedonia during Paul's stay in Ephesus than during Paul's imprisonment in Rome.[43] An Ephesian provenance for Philippians seems slightly more probable. As I see it, then, this is how it all stands:

For Rome:

- There is a strong possibility that Philippians was written in Rome and, if so, Timothy's presence with Paul in Rome is thereby established since he was a cosender of the letter to the Philippians. The Paul–Timothy–Rome connection can then be linked with the letters to Philemon and to the Colossians.

- The theology of Colossians appears to be "developed" in some sense.

- There is no clear reference to an Ephesian imprisonment and it is hard to place John Mark in Ephesus.

For Ephesus:

- An Ephesian setting for Philippians remains highly probable.

- There is no clear reference to Timothy in Rome during Paul's imprisonment there, but we can place him easily in Ephesus.

- An imprisonment in Ephesus makes for a more plausible scenario regarding the movements of Onesimus and others to and from Colossae.

43. Cf. Thielman 2003.

- Colossae may have been destroyed in 61–62 CE leaving Paul no one to even write to.

The marginally less problematic of these options then is the Ephesian provenance.[44] I surmise that the epistle to Philemon was written by Paul himself during an imprisonment in Ephesus (ca. 55–57 CE) and Philemon subsequently discharged Onesimus to Paul's service where he became thereafter part of Paul's entourage. Colossians was written cooperatively by Paul and his coworkers (Col 1:1; 4:7–17) from Ephesus and was delivered by Tychicus and Onesimus. Ephesians was written by a secretary of Paul at Paul's behest and composed on the basis of Colossians in order to be given to the Pauline churches of Asia Minor, including Ephesus and Laodicea, as the letter carriers passed through those regions on their way to deliver the correspondence to Colossae. In editorial language, Paul is the author of Philemon, the managing editor and chief contributor to Colossians, and the commissioning editor of Ephesians.

The Colossian Philosophy

Another confusing matter is the nature of the Colossian "philosophy."[45] We have no direct account of the philosophy by the teachers themselves, but are reliant entirely upon what Paul says about them, directly and indirectly, in Colossians. What Paul wrote against the philosophy is itself based on what he was told about them from others and is admixed with some general exhortations that could apply to many doctrinal intrusions among Christian groups. It is hard to determine the precise contours of the philosophy since Paul speaks of them explicitly only at limited points (2:4, 8, 16–23) and elsewhere perhaps only implicitly (1:15–20, 22–23; 2:2–3; 3:1–2).[46] There is also the problem of trying to understand what kind of religious label the philosophy fits into. J. J. Gunther listed forty-four different identifications of Paul's opponents in Colossae in his 1973

44. I have changed my mind on this since Bird 2008a: 65. Note also the hesitancy of Moule 1957: 24; and Dunn 1996: 41.

45. I prefer the term "philosophy" since that is the word used to describe the viewpoint that Paul is opposing in Colossians (2:8) and other terms like "error" or "heresy" presuppose later standards of orthodoxy.

46. On the methodology for trying to identify Paul's opponents in Colossae see Sumney 1993; Wolter 1993: 156; DeMaris 1994: 41–45; Arnold 1996: 4; Stettler 2005: 172.

monograph, and more are continually added.[47] Morna Hooker proposed that there actually was no heresy or false teachers in Colossae and Paul merely writes a general admonition to urge the congregation there not to conform to the beliefs and practices of their Jewish and pagan neighbors.[48] But the portrayal of the philosophy seems far too specific and the use of the indefinite pronouns suggests that Paul genuinely did have some group or individual in mind (2:8, 16, 18). Others advocate not a Jewish or pagan threat to the Colossian church, but a Christian heresy based on the mystery religions,[49] the Ebionites,[50] or a syncretism involving the Christian gospel, Judaism, and Hellenistic cosmology.[51] While there might be some grounds for suggesting that the philosophy has begun impacting the Colossians (e.g., 2:19), for the most part it seems that it remains an external and decidedly non-Christian threat. Paul would be unlikely to commend the Colossians' faithfulness and steadfastness if they had succumbed to the philosophy (1:4; 2:5). Never are the "teachers" in Colossae charged with denying Jesus, perverting the gospel, or with being "false" as Paul alleges of his opponents elsewhere (see Gal 1:7; 2:4–5; 5:2–4; 2 Cor 11:4; cf. Jude 4; 1 John 4:1–2; Rev 2:2).

47. Gunther 1973; and see surveys in Francis 1975; Stettler 2005; Smith 2006: 19–38.

48. Hooker 1973; but see response by Gnilka 1980: 163–64 n. 4. Calvin (1979a: 132–33) saw Paul confronting worldly philosophy on the one hand with its reference to "stars, fate, the trifles of a like nature" and the Jews on the other hand who urged "observance of their ceremonies" and "had raised up many mists with a view of throwing Christ into the shade." These Jews are clearly Jewish Christians for Calvin, and he says that they tried to "mix up Christ with Moses, and might retain the shadows of the law along with the gospel." Throughout the commentary he calls them "false apostles." At the same time Calvin saw these false teachers as Hellenistic to some extent and concerned with speculations contained in the books of Dionysius on the Celestial Hierarchy stemming from the Platonic school. Calvin emphasizes at length Paul's critique of Jewish ceremonies (1979a: 181–82, 188–89), which he sees pregnant even in the "elements" (2:8) and "written code" (2:14).

49. Cf. e.g., Dibelius 1975: 99.

50. Baur 2003 [1873–75]: 2.28–32.

51. Cf. e.g., Lincoln (2000: 567) who writes: "[T]he proponent(s) of the teaching have taken a number of elements from Judaism and the Christian gospel and linked these with typical cosmological concerns from the Hellenistic world. It is quite plausible that a Hellenistic Jew who had left the synagogue to join a Pauline congregation or a Gentile convert who had had some previous contact with the synagogue would advocate such a philosophy, and the writer evidently was concerned that it might appeal to others among his preponderantly Gentile Christian readers." Similarly, see Arnold 1996: 228–29.

The philosophy was clearly indebted to Judaism in some form given the references to the Sabbath (2:16), circumcision (2:11), and food laws (2:21). However, the references to the "powers" (1:16; 2:8, 10, 15), the "worship of angels" (2:18), asceticism (2:21–23), festivals (2:16), and wisdom (1:9, 2:3, 23; 3:16) could derive from a number of different religious and philosophical systems. If we add to that the melting pot of religions, philosophies, and magic in Phrygia (interior Asia Minor) where syncretism was common and Jewish acculturation inevitable, it further complicates our ability to pin down concretely the philosophy to any one particular philosophical school or known religious movement. Even so, three main options present themselves for consideration.

First, the "philosophy" could have derived from one of the Hellenistic philosophical schools of Pythagoreanism,[52] Middle Platonism,[53] or even Cynicism.[54] The problem is, however, that "philosophy" is such a broad category and many of the philosophies of the ancient world (Stoicism, Pythagoreanism, Cynicism, etc.) often overlapped in their metaphysical understanding of the world. Moreover, while it is conceivable that Jewish philosophers could admix Hellenistic philosophy to their system of belief, it is less likely that non-Jews would add Jewish rituals denoting Jewish identity to their religious practices, especially Sabbath keeping and circumcision.

Second, the philosophers might be advocating a syncretistic amalgam of Judaism and indigenous Phrygian practices of magic, mysteries, and angel veneration. Nearly all commentators regard the philosophy as a syncretism of some form.[55] Philo appears to complain about the infiltration of syncretism among the Jews of Alexandria, which poses a similar analogy.[56] Martin Hengel and Anna Maria Schwemer point out that around one third of the extant magical papyri and amulets are based on Jewish elements.[57] We also know from later papyri and patristic evidence that even many Christians were willing to use magic spells for particular

---

52. Schweizer 1982: 81, 129–33, 136–37, 151.

53. DeMaris 1994; Kooten 2003: 143–46.

54. Martin 1996.

55. Cf. Bruce 1957: 166–67; Lohse 1971: 18, 128; Martin 1973: 18–19; O'Brien 1982: xxxviii; Barth and Blanke 1994: 38; Lincoln 2000: 563–68; and esp. Arnold 1996.

56. Philo *Spec.* 1.315–16.

57. Hengel and Schwemer 1997: 70.

ends.[58] Furthermore, some Jews were known to practice magic as evidenced by Bar-Jesus/Elymas who, according to Acts, was something of a personal attendant or chaplain to Sergius Paulus on the island of Cyprus (Acts 13:6–12). The second century Christian polemicist Celsus mentioned Jews "who worship angels and are addicted to sorcery of which Moses was their teacher."[59] Clinton Arnold has shown how angels were important in ancient magic for protection and petitions.[60] There is an inscription from Phrygia concerning a Jewish lady, Julia Severa, who was a synagogue benefactor and a priestess of the imperial cult.[61]

At the same time, the argument for a syncretistic Judaism in Asia Minor can be overstated. Josephus records that most Jews in Asia Minor strictly observed the laws about food and festivals and came into conflict with their Gentile neighbors because of their faithfulness to the Jewish way of life.[62] Paul Trebilco states, "No evidence has arisen from this study to suggest that Judaism in Asia minor was syncretistic or had been compromised by paganism."[63] Similar is F. F. Bruce: "Some outward conformity with pagan customs on the part of influential Jews in Phrygia may be taken as established; but it would be precarious to draw conclusions from this about forms of syncretism that might be reflected in the beliefs and practices deprecated in Paul's Epistle to the Colossians."[64] We should also be aware of the looseness of the term "syncretism." What counts as syncretism? For instance, according to the Mishnah tractate ʿ*Abodah Zarah* a Jew is permitted to make and sell idols for a living (*m.* ʿ*Abod. Zar.* 1.8). If one believes that Zeus is another name of Yahweh, is that syncretism or pluralism (*Ep. Arist.* 16)? Some Jewish apocalyptic writings could venerate angels like Metratron, the "little Yahwheh," but without actually compromising their Jewish beliefs *in toto* (*3 En.* 10:3; 12:5; 17:1–3; 30:1; *b. Sanh.* 38b). In relation to Colossians, I would make two further points. First, there is no reference to magic, amulets, spells, calling on angels, or initiation rites in pagan temples. Second, there is a difference between

---

58. Cf. Meyer and Smith 1994; Arnold 1996: 83–97, 238–43; Busch 2007.

59. Origen *Cels.* 1.26.

60. Arnold 1996: 20–31.

61. See discussion and references in Bruce 1984a: 7; Trebilco 1991: 58–59.

62. Cf. e.g., Josephus *Ant.* 14.261.

63. Trebilco 1991: 142; cf. Dunn 1995: 156.

64. Bruce 1984a: 7.

syncretism and acculturation. Colossians exhibits the telltale signs of a set of Jewish teachings expressed in the idiom and categories of Hellenism. Yet Hellenism itself can either flatten out or reinforce Jewish distinctives as exposure to a secondary culture forces one to either absorb or deflect external influences.

Third, the philosophy is conceivably a form of Judaism that is being commended to the Colossians. Judaism could also be described as a philosophy in apologetic literature.[65] Josephus describes the various Jewish sects as philosophies[66] and he can even refer to the Jewish religion as a form of national philosophy.[67] Philo represents Judaism as achieving the highest ideals of Hellenistic philosophy.[68] What also indicates Jewish adversaries is the injunction in 2:16–17, where the triadic formula of festivals, new moons, and Sabbaths occurs in the Septuagint and represents the commandments of the Torah (law of Moses). The references to circumcision (2:11, 3:11, and 4:11) imply that while circumcision itself was probably not the presenting issue, nonetheless, it was crucial in identifying Paul's opponents. What is more, there are a number of similarities between the teachers in Colossae and the proselytizers in Galatia and how both are engaged by Paul. The philosophy is touted as an oppressive spiritual force in much the same way that Paul likens the law in Galatians to hostile spiritual powers (Col 2:8, 14–15; Gal 4:9–11). In Colossians, as in Galatians, the erroneous beliefs required Paul to shore up the integrity of Gentile Christian identity without the need to take on law observance (Col 3:11; Gal 3:28). In Colossians as in Galatians, Paul exhorts that one does not require Torah to facilitate righteous living (Col 2:23–3:17; Gal 5:13–15). In Colossians as in Galatians, freedom from the designs of the Colossian philosophers and from the Galatian proselytizers is indebted to dying with Messiah and being baptized into Messiah (Col 2:12; 3:3; Gal 3:26–27). Colossians and Galatians both refer to the freedom of the Christian from circumcision and festivals (Col 2:11–12, 16; Gal 5:2; 6:12–15; 4:10) and refer to deliverance from evil powers (Col 1:13–14; Gal 1:4). In light of this, it seems that Paul is evidently negating the value of Jewish boundary markers and lessening the social and religious function of the

65. 4 Macc 5:22; *Ep. Arist.* 30–31.

66. *J. W.* 2.119, 166; *Ant.* 18.11, 25.

67. *Ant.* 1.18; 16.398; *Ag. Ap.* 1.181; 2.47.

68. Cf. *Opif.* 8.128; *Migr.* 34; *Somn.* 1.226; 2.244; *Mos.* 2.2; *Spec.* 1.32, 37; 3.185–91; *Legat.* 156, 245, 318.

law as it stands as a threat to the integrity of Jesus-believing Gentiles and involves a devaluing of the preeminence of the Messiah.

But what type of Judaism was Paul engaging? A hybrid Jewish Gnosticism could be conceivable if Colossians was written late in the first century or in the early second century.[69] Yet Colossians was not likely to have been composed so late, and the philosophy lacks the anti-cosmic dualism that was at the root of Gnosticism whereby the creation of the material world is attributed to the act of a malevolent demiurge. Over a hundred years ago J. B. Lightfoot suggested that the "heresy" had an affinity with Essenism and Gnosticism since the Essenes had a tendency towards mysticism.[70] The discovery of the Dead Sea Scrolls, arguably stemming from an Essene sect, provided further grounds for links between the Colossian philosophy and the Essenes. Pierre Benoit writes, "A return to the Mosaic law by circumcision, rigid observance concerning diet and the calendar, speculations about the angelic powers: all this is part and parcel of the doctrines of Qumran."[71] The parallels between the philosophy and Josephus's account of the Essenes and with selected portions of the Qumran scrolls are undeniable. However, there remains the absence of any evidence that the Essenes were in Phrygia or the Lycus Valley. The asceticism and mysticism of the philosophy could also comport with a number of other Jewish religious strains, including *merkabah* mystics or apocalyptic sects.

I want to suggest, in line with a number of researchers, that the background to the philosophy lies in Jewish mysticism.[72] First, F. F. Bruce noted the affinities of the Colossian philosophy with *merkabah* mysticism.[73] *Merkabah* mysticism was a Jewish movement that got its name from its concern with visions of the heavenly chariot (*mrkbh*) that was with God during Ezekiel's glorious vision (Ezek 1:4–28). Visions of God's throne and angelic worship were granted to those who undertook rigorous adherence to the Mosaic law with periods of asceticism and purifica-

---

69. Cf. e.g., Bruce 1957: 166; Lohse 1971: 129; Bornkamm 1975: 130; Pokorný 1991: 117–21.

70. Lightfoot 1879: 82–114; but see criticisms in Yamauchi 1964; Lohse 1971: 128–29; Barth and Blanke 1994: 379; Smith 2006: 21–24.

71. Benoit 1968: 17.

72. Cf. e.g., Francis 1975; Evans 1982; O'Brien 1982: xxxviii; Rowland 1983; Bruce 1984c; Sappington 1991; Sumney 1993: 387–88; Dunn 1995; 1996: 174; Garland 1998: 27; Roberts 1998; Smith 2006; Talbert 2007: 219; Witherington 2007: 165–66.

73. Bruce 1984c: 201–4.

tion as a form of preparation for such visions. Eventually this led to what the later rabbis called the "two powers in heaven" heresy, since the name Yahweh was said to include two deities. There is no doubt that our sources on *merkabah* mysticism postdate Paul, nonetheless, similar visionary experiences, ascents to heaven, and interest in heavenly worship are attested pre-70 CE (e.g., Pss 29:1–2; 148:1–2; 2 Cor 12:1–4; *1 En.* 14:8–23; 4Q405; *Apoc. Ab.* 17:1–21; *Apoc. Zeph.* 8:3–4; *Ascen. Isa.* 7:13—9:33), which provide a backdrop to Col 2:18.[74]

Second, adherence to regulations of the Mosaic law can be linked to the veneration and appeasement of angels. The law was said to have been given *to* Moses *by* God *through* angels (see Gal 3:19; Acts 7:53; Heb 2:2). As such, keeping the law becomes a tribute to the angels and disobedience to the precepts of the law can result in judgment from angelic beings. There is clear evidence that some Jews taught that circumcision and obedience to the law could protect someone from evil angels.[75] Thus, the need to follow the regulations of the Torah in Col 2:14, 16–17 is perhaps connected to the heavenly jurisdiction of the "thrones" and "authorities" who are angelic beings that demand observance of the law. Paul argues in turn that there is no need to placate those cosmic entities whom the Messiah has supremacy over (1:16; 2:8–10) and has subjugated (2:15).

Third, the references to asceticism, visions, and the worship of angels underscore the mystical aspect of the philosophy even more. This is apparent in 2:18 where there are those who "insist" or "delight"[76] upon ascetic practices and self-abasement. This self-mortification probably pertains to fasting as an expression of humility (Pss 35:13; 69:10; Isa 58:3, 5; Jdt 4:9). The self-deprivation of fasting was often a means to visionary experiences (Dan 10:2–3; *Apoc. Ab.* 9:7–10; 12:1–2; *T. Isaac* 4:1–6; 5:4; *4 Ezra* 5:13, 20; 6:35; 9:23–25; *2 Bar.* 43:3; *Gk. Apoc. Ezra* 1:2–7) and this may have enabled participants to have, or claim to have had, visions of

---

74. Cf. discussion in Smith 2006: 38–73.

75. CD 16.4–6 and the "Angel of Obstruction"; *Jub.* 15:28–32 and the spirits who "rule so that they might be led astray." According to Hippolytus (*Haer.* 9.11) a Jewish Christian group called the Elchasai urged keeping the Sabbath because "There exist wicked stars of impiety . . . Honour the day of thee Sabbath, since that day is one of those during which prevails (the power) of these stars." Note also the incantation of 4Q510 1:4–6 for warding off evil angels and spirits: "And I, the Sage, declare the grandeur of his radiance in order to frighten and terr[ify] all the spirits of the ravaging angels and the bastard spirits, demons, Liliths, owls, and [jackals . . .]."

76. Or else *thelōn* is adverbial and means "intentionally disqualifying" (BDF §148.2).

ascents to heaven to behold angelic worship (e.g., Isa 6:2–3; Dan 7:10; Luke 2:14; Rev 4–5). That is why this "self-abasement" is closely linked to the "worship of angels" and going into detail about "visions which he has seen."

But what precisely is the "worship of angels"? Is it the worship of angels themselves or worship with the angels? Traditionally, it has been taken as an objective genitive, meaning worship directed at the angels, which could be occasioned by the view of angels as divine mediators, lesser deities, or stemming from an angel cult in Phyrgia. It is common today to argue that it is a subjective genitive and refers to worship performed by the angels. That corresponds with the narration found in various apocalypses where prophets and saints of old are translated to God's throne and participate in the praises of heaven.[77] The evidence from the Qumran scrolls also shows that angelic worship was much coveted and the liturgy of the sectarians was thought to include the presence of the angels (e.g., 1QH 3:21–22; 1QM 7:4–6; 1QSa 2:8–9; 1QSb 4:25–26). In particular, the *Songs of the Sabbath Sacrifice* (4Q400–5) describe the praise of angels in the heavenly sanctuary where the angels are assembled in military formation and provide anthems of divine blessing to God:

> The [Cheru]bim fall before Him and bless Him; as they arise, the quiet voice of God [is heard], followed by a tumult of joyous praise. As they unfold their wings, God's q[uiet] voice is heard again. The Cherubim bless the image of the chariot-throne that appears above the firmament, [then] they joyously acclaim the [splend]or of the luminous firmament that spreads beneath His glorious seat. As the wheel-beings advance, holy angels come and go. Between His chariot-throne's glorious [w]heels appears something like an utterly holy spiritual fire. All around are what appear to be streams of fire, resembling electrum, and [sh]ining handiwork comprising wondrous colors embroidered together, pure and glorious. The spirits of the living [go]dlike beings move to and fro perpetually, following the glory of the two [wo]ndrous chariots. A quiet voice of blessing accompanies the tumult of their movement, and they bless the Holy One each time they retrace their steps. When they rise up, they do so wondrously, and when they settle down, they [sta]nd still. The sound of joyous rejoicing falls silent, and the qui[et] blessing of God spreads through all the camps of the di-

---

77. *Apoc. Ab.* 17–18; *2 Bar.* 2:2; 3:1–2; *T. Levi* 3:4–8; *T. Job* 48–50; *Apoc. Zeph.* 8:3–4; *Ascen. Isa.* 7:37; 8:17; 9:28–34 (Smith 2006: 126).

> vine beings. The sound of prais[es] . . . coming out of each of their
> divisions on [both] sides, and each of the mustered troops rejoices,
> one by one in order of rank . . .[78]

Also central to the discussion is the meaning of the Greek word *thrēskeia*
in Col 2:18. F. O. Francis argues that in 4 Macc 5:7 and Josephus *Ant.*
12.253 the word *thrēskeia* is used for the "worship" that belongs to the
Jews, not worship of the Jews. He applies it similarly to Col 2:18 as meaning "worship" belonging to the angels, i.e., worship performed by the
angels.[79] Clinton Arnold correctly notes, however, that "A survey of the
usage of *thrēskeia* fails to turn up one example of a divine being, or a
typical object of worship . . . related to *thrēskeia* in the genitive case that
should be taken as a subjective genitive."[80] While this may be true, we
have already documented evidence of seers claiming to have partaken
of heavenly worship with angelic beings. What is more, Arnold's otherwise erudite study flounders on the observation that *thrēskeia* was not
used in any of the magical incantations involving angels that he cites and
there is no reference to incantations over angelic names in Colossians.[81]
Alternatively, Loren Stuckenbruck points out there is no need to choose
absolutely between an objective genitive ("worshipping the angels")
and a subjective genitive ("worship performed by the angels") because
if someone is insisting on the benefits attained by seeing angelic worship, then they are also attributing something special and majestic to the
angels themselves. The problem is not only the superfluity of the ritual
and vision for the believer, but also the temptation to venerate angels encountered in the ascent.[82] In fact, gaining access to worship of the angels
by ascetic practices and appeasing the angels by law observance are not
mutually exclusive.

A further factor in favor of defining the philosophy as tied with
Jewish mysticism is the use of the word *embateuō* in 2:18. The word,
though ambiguous, seems to be linked to visionary reports of "entering into" or "going into detail about" heavenly ascents and what is seen
therein (see *1 En.* 14:9).[83] Persons in Colossae are perhaps boasting about

78. 4Q405 frags. xxi–xxii, 6–14 (trans. Wise, Abegg, and Cook).

79. Francis 1975: 180.

80. Arnold 1996: 91.

81. Cf. Arnold 1996: 93–95.

82. Stuckenbruck 1995: 117–19; cf. Rowland 1983: 117.

83. Some have argued that *embateuō* was a technical term in the mystery cults for ini-

the worship of the angels that they have seen upon entrance into the heavenly realm and subsequently venerating the angels that accompanied them in their tour of the heavenly court. A plausible scenario, then, is that the teachers advocated the necessity of ascetic practices leading to visionary experiences resulting in one sharing in the angelic liturgies of heaven, submitting to angelic "rulers and authorities," who exercised some form of power over them through law observance, and translating all of this into their every day pattern of life (2:8–10, 16–23). The role of angels in the Colossian philosophy may not be clear-cut since their roles in veneration, mediation, or domination could overlap. What seems likely is that the Colossian philosophy represents a combination of the ascetic-mystical piety of Jewish apocalypticism with its emphasis on visionary experiences of heavenly ascents (an incipient form of *merkabah* mysticism), the dualism of Hellenistic cosmology and anthropology, and *perhaps* the veneration of angels influenced by local pagan folk religions involving appeal to angels through magic; all of these are possibilities for comprising elements of the philosophy.

Another element of the Colossian philosophy that I wish to advocate is its tacit missionary function. One or more persons from Colossae or the Lycus Valley is commending Judaism to the Gentile Christians in Colossae by using the religious ritual of ascetic-mystic Judaism and the language of Hellenistic philosophy (most likely Stoicism of some form) as a means of attracting them to it. Harald Hegermann argues that the Colossians were being exposed to Jewish missionary propaganda,[84] and while I reject the idea of widespread Jewish missionary activity, nonetheless, I think here it has something going for it. Jewish communities did attract proselytes and many Jews wrote philosophical defenses of their

---

tiation rites and its presence in Colossians means that some of the Gentile converts were previously involved in the mystery cults. This is based largely on an inscription from the Apollos temple at Claros 30 km north of Ephesus, which uses the word *embateuō* three times (Dibelius 1975; Arnold 1996: 104–57). The problem is that in the various witnesses to the mystery rites *embateuō* is never used alone and always includes the words *muēsis* or *epopteia* for expressing the reception of the mysteries. This combination of words is entirely lacking from Col 2:18–23, which evacuates the argument for a "technical" usage of *embateuō*. A far better background for *embateuō* is Jewish mystical ascents to heaven for worship with the angels (Sappington 1991: 156–68; Rowland 1983: 76; Evans 1982: 198).

84. Hegermann 1961: 162; cf. Stettler 2005: 196. Discussed further in Bird [forthcoming].

faith for largely Jewish audiences but potentially for Gentile readers as well. Many Gentiles did convert to Judaism and in numbers high enough to alarm the cultural elites.[85] Gentile adherents to Jewish ways, sometimes known as God-fearers, do not seem to have been an infrequent occurrence either.[86] James Dunn argues that the Colossian philosophy represents the *apologia* (philosophical defense) of a local synagogue responding to the rise of a form of messianic Judaism in their immediate circle.[87] If the best type of defense is offense, then perhaps a circle of Jewish teachers from a local synagogue immersed in Jewish mystical traditions and Hellenistic thought have come into contact with Christians in Colossae and are commending this form of "Judaism" to them. Their criticism of Christianity and Jesus Christ may even be benign in down playing rather than denying him a heavenly role. They condemn those who do not keep the regulations of Torah, they claim a share in the inheritance of Israel, and insist that the Colossian Christians undertake the ascetic rigor required for heavenly visions.[88] This scenario provides an appropriate background to the Colossian philosophy and explains the socio-rhetorical dynamics of the letter. This accounts for the Jewish character of the philosophy as well as the Hellenistic terminology in which it is expressed. The philosophy, as it is written about in the letter to the Colossians, arguably represents an attempt by one or more Jewish individuals to recruit Christian Gentiles to a form of Jewish belief and practice through a highly contextualized missionary approach. The absence of a concerted polemic against circumcision (though perhaps implied in 2:11; 3:11; and 4:11) by Paul may be said to count against that hypothesis. But I suggest that the polemical references to circumcision, spiritual or physical, could hardly be heard as any other than an intra-Jewish debate stemming from factional rivalries over the nature and boundaries of Jewish identity. What is more, not all forms of Jewish missionary activity were necessarily said to be after "full" converts. Some Jewish perspectives on conversion did not require circumcision (see especially Josephus *Ant.* 20.41 and Philo *QE* 2.2) and only sought partial adherents and philosophical respect for its beliefs and practices in a wider intellectual forum. Whereas Lohse argues that the

85. Seneca *De Superstitione*; cited in Augustine *Civ.* 6.11; Tacitus *Hist.* 5.5; Juvenal *Sat.* 14.96–106.

86. Cf. Acts 10:2, 22, 35; 13:16, 26, 43, 50; 16:14; 17:4, 17; 18:7.

87. Dunn 1995; 1996: 34.

88. Cf. Stettler 2005: 193.

sacramental initiation was made more attractive by dressing it up in a Jewish term,[89] I think the reverse holds, viz., an essentially Jewish religious tradition is being dressed in a garb of Hellenistic philosophy and language, thus appealing to Gentile believers who were formerly pagans in the religious smorgasbord of the Lycus Valley.

THE SITUATION BEHIND THE EPISTLE TO PHILEMON

So far we have tentatively concluded that the letter to Philemon was written during 55–56 CE during Paul's imprisonment in Ephesus. It was composed due to the estrangement between Onesimus and Philemon, which, after Paul's intervention, resulted in Philemon releasing Onesimus to Paul's care and service. Some time thereafter, Onesimus and Tychicus were dispatched to the Lycus Valley to deliver the letters to the Colossians and Laodiceans (Ephesians).[90]

It is hard to say much about Paul's relationship to Philemon and Onesimus because we know very little of the specifics. Philemon was evidently a well-to-do Christian in a small Phyrigan town of the Lycus Valley in Asia Minor, he was a slave owner, and a church met in his house which was presumably led by himself, his wife Apphia, and Archippus. He seems to have shared some kind of partnership/fellowship (*koinōnon*) with Paul (v. 17), which elsewhere means becoming partners in ministry by sharing material needs (see Acts 2:42; Phil 1:5; 2:1). Paul also says that Philemon owes him his very own self, perhaps suggesting that Paul was significant in Philemon's conversion and now the apostle seeks a mutual benefit from this relationship (v. 20). Onesimus is known from Colossians as "one of yourselves" and he later travelled with Tychicus to Colossae (Col 4:7–9). He was a slave who had come to Paul, or perhaps he sought out Epaphras and Paul together because they were esteemed by his master and could mediate between them. Or else maybe one of Paul's associates found him hiding somewhere in want of food and shelter. Sometime during

89. Lohse 1971: 130.

90. About Philemon and Colossians we have already noted that: (1) they are both written during a Pauline imprisonment, (2) they have the same coauthor in Timothy, (3) they share the same list of Pauline coworkers in the closing greetings, and (4) there is no mention of the Philemon/Onesimus tension in Colossians, which led us to infer that the rift had been healed and Onesimus is called a "faithful and beloved brother" implying that he had proven himself in service. Thus, the letter to Philemon probably precedes that written to the Colossians by some time.

Onesimus's period of respite and sanctuary with Paul, he was converted to Christian faith (v. 10). Why he had not converted earlier as part of Philemon's household is a good question but one we cannot answer.

What is the situation behind the letter? There are several options to consider.[91] First, there is the traditional view that Onesimus had simply run away from Philemon most probably because he had damaged goods or stolen something leaving his master Philemon out of pocket (vv. 11, 18). Onesimus then sought shelter with Paul, a respected friend of the master, and Paul pleads to Philemon to forgive Onesimus his transgression and hopefully allow him to remain in Paul's retinue. But there are further factors for consideration that might count against this proposal, such as the observation that Paul never uses the words *phygas*, *draptēs*, or *fugitivus* as terms to describe Onesimus as a slave taken to flight. Nor does he ever refer to the dire punishments that await a returned fugitive slave. Normally runaways try to vanish, so why would a runaway slave flee to his master's friend and run the risk of being turned over to authorities? Maybe Onesimus had a change of mind or knew that his capture was imminent, but these are speculations to account for the fact that a runaway slave is now in the company of a friend of his master. Moreover, nowhere in the letter is the precise reason for Onesimus's sudden departure ever given, and running away is only one possibility, which is more ordinarily assumed than proven.

A second option is that Onesimus is not a runaway slave, but is rather a slave who is in some measure of domestic trouble with his master and seeks the intervention of an *amicus domini* (friend of the master) to intercede for him in hope of being restored back to favored status in Philemon's household. In this sense, the letter to Philemon is roughly analogous to the letter that Pliny the Younger sent to Sabinus to intercede on behalf of a freedman to his master.[92]

91. Cf. Fitzmyer 2000: 17–24.

92. Pliny *Ep.* 9.21: "To Sabianus. The freedman of yours with whom you said you were angry has been to me, flung himself at my feet, and clung to me as if I were you. He begged my help with many tears, though he left a good deal unsaid; in short, he convinced me of his genuine penitence. I believe he has reformed, because he realizes that he did wrong. You are angry, I know, and I know too that your anger was deserved, but mercy wins most praise when there was just cause for anger. You loved the man once, and I hope you will love again, but it is sufficient for the moment if you allow yourself to be appeased. You can always be angry again if he deserves it, and will have more excuse if you were once placated. Make some concession to his youth, his tears and your own

A third view is that the slave Onesimus was sent to Paul by the church of Colossae to provide provisions for the apostle, but Paul writes back asking that Onesimus be permanently released to his team of coworkers to assist in evangelization. Sarah Winter bases this largely on the high frequency of commercial terminology in the letter as Paul seeks to have Onesimus break all formal and legal ties with Philemon's household.[93]

Finally, a fourth perspective is that Onesimus was not a slave at all, but only a brother of Philemon, and Paul seeks to reconcile two estranged brothers. Key to this position is understanding "as a slave" metaphorically, whereas "as a beloved brother" is not metaphorical (v. 16). Paul refers to the physical kinship of Onesimus and Philemon "in the flesh" as well as a fictive kinship "in the Lord" as the basis of their reconciliation. A. D. Callahan writes: "When Paul exhorted Philemon to receive Onesimus no longer as a slave, he was there commanding the former to desist in treating the latter as though he were beyond the pale of fraternal entitlements to love, honor, and respect . . . In this short, diplomatic epistle Paul attempted deftly to heal a rift not between errant slave and irate master, but between estranged Christian brothers."[94] In light of this I conclude:

(a) Against option four that Onesimus and Philemon are brothers is that the letter has far too much gravity and pathos for Paul simply to be urging Philemon to treat Onesimus as a *beloved* brother. Fraternal love is a major theme, but it exists between the two now only in light of Onesimus's conversion. Paul seems to use a different form of exhortation when he seeks reconciliation of equal persons within a community (e.g., Phil 4:2; 2 Cor 2:5–11). It is the social inequality between the two, deliberately complicated by Onesimus's conversion,[95] that is the problem in the reconciliation.

(b) Against option three that Paul seeks to have Onesimus released to his service is that this view lacks any reasonable explanation of the disruption between Onesimus and Philemon that is apparent in verses 15–19, and particularly the fact that the separation could have implied

---

kind heart, and do not torment him or yourself any longer—anger can only be a torment to your gentle self" (trans. B. Radice [LCL]).

93. Cf. Winter 1987.

94. Callahan 1993: 371.

95. On Onesimus's conversion we have to ask, did Onesimus go to Paul to gain leverage over his master and was a safe return to Philemon a contributing factor in Onesimus's conversion to faith in Jesus (see Barclay 1996: 102)?

that Philemon might never receive Onesimus back at all (v. 15). Did Philemon or Archippus think that by sending Onesimus to Paul on an errand or with supplies that they were thereby running the risk of never seeing him again? I would doubt it.

(c) The first option, the view that Onesimus was a runaway slave, explains the language of being "separated" (v. 15), "wronged," and "owed" (v. 18). The reference to "as a slave" is probably real (v. 16); that Paul needs Philemon's consent before enlisting Onesimus among his cohort of co-workers implies a slave-master relationship between the two (vv. 13–14). Yet this view lacks the expected references to fugitive status, there is no mention of the severity of punishment that could await a runaway slave, it begs the question of why Onesimus went to Paul at all rather than vanish entirely, and finally, no explicit circumstance for Onesimus's flight is given, which must give cause for thought.

(d) I conclude that the second option is the most probable, and that Onesimus journeyed to Ephesus from Colossae to have Paul mediate between him and his master over some matter that is now public before the Colossian church. Onesimus has become a believer as a result of the encounter, which, in tandem with Paul's religious authority, adds further reason for Philemon to respond favorably to Onesimus and to heed Paul's request. The urgent qualification that needs to be made here is that Philemon's perception of Onesimus's absence may not accord with Onesimus's actual intentions in going to Paul. The technical legal distinction between a runaway slave and a slave absent from duty and absconded to his master's superior, may not exist in the mind of an irate slave owner.[96] Either way, Paul agrees to be an advocate for Onesimus to Philemon in order to effect reconciliation between them and to secure a better future for them beyond the normal slave-master relationship.

PAUL AND SLAVERY

More sensitively we have to ask: did Paul endorse slavery or was he at least complicit to its continuing operation?[97] The mere mention of slavery conjures up feelings and thoughts that are so clearly an affront to our modern

---

96. Cf. further Barclay 1996: 101–2; Harrill 1999.

97. On slavery in the New Testament and antiquity see Guzlow 1969; Keener 1992: 188–207; Barth and Blanke 2000: 1–102; Harrill 2005; and the history of interpretation of Paul and slavery in Byron 2008.

moral sensibilities. We desperately want Paul to speak out directly against it and we are scandalized that he did not do so. Space prohibits us from entering into a lengthy discussion of slavery in antiquity. By one definition a slave was a person who did not have the right of refusal. Some people voluntarily sold themselves into slavery in order to avoid a deathly poverty, and many slaves enjoyed good living conditions during their service and were even rewarded with emancipation. Yet in the ancient world a slave was regarded as a piece of human property and susceptible to manifold forms of abuse and exploitation (particularly vulnerable were women and children). Many were forced into slavery as a result of capture from war—both combatants and civilians—and some were born into slavery. In major urban centers up to one third of the population were slaves. Four points need to be mentioned:[98] (1) Slavery was indelibly part of the social structure, welfare system, and economic activity of the ancient world and no one seems to have envisaged the operation of society without the institution of slavery. While the moral treatment of slaves was discussed on a philosophical plane, the fact of slavery was never debated and its necessity was simply assumed. (2) In the absence of a modern democracy and libertarian ethics it would have been impossible to lodge an effective and successful political protest against slavery. (3) The most effective means of ameliorating the slave's plight was through just and kind treatment by a master, with the hope of manumission at a future point, and the prospect of remaining under the master's patronage and provision as a freedman or freedwoman. (4) In 1 Cor 7:21 ("Were you a slave when you were called? Don't let it trouble you—although if you can gain your freedom, do so") Paul seems to urge slaves not to accept the status quo, but seek to improve their condition and achieve their freedom where possible. Moreover, in the epistle to Philemon, Paul urges Philemon to accept Onesimus in a way that radically alters the slave-master relationship. It is their fictive kinship as brothers in Messiah and coworkers for the kingdom that transcends societal norms and also transforms their attitudes, actions, and responses towards each other with a decidedly Christian ethic. F. F. Bruce notes that the epistle to Philemon "brings us into an atmosphere in which the institution of slavery could only wilt and die."[99] Paul was no William Wilberforce, but without Paul we might never have had William Wilberforce.

98. Dunn 1996: 306–7.
99. Bruce 1977: 401.

COLOSSIANS

LETTER OPENING AND GREETING (1:1–2)

> [1] Paul, an Apostle of Messiah Jesus through the will of God and Timothy our brother. [2] To the holy and faithful brothers and sisters in Messiah in Colossae. Grace to you and peace from God our Father.

The letter begins with a standard epistolary prescript detailing the sender and recipient. At the head of the letter stands **Paul, an Apostle of Messiah Jesus**. The mention of **Paul** introduces the apostle as the author (or coauthor) of the communication. Paul did not establish the church in Colossae, but he would no doubt have been known to the Colossian assembly through Epaphras who was probably sent by Paul to establish house churches in the Lycus Valley (Col 1:7; 4:12; Phlm 23). Paul's evangelistic activities and hardships faced in Ephesus (1 Cor 15:32; 16:8; Acts 18:19; 19:1–41; 20:17–38) would have been among the things for which he was known. The letter stands as a substitute then for his personal presence and is also all the more important given the current absence of Epaphras and the uncertainties surrounding the effectiveness of the ministry of Archippus (Col 4:17; Phlm 2). As usual, Paul identifies himself as an **apostle**, and *apostolos* means "one who is sent" or an authorized emissary of a third party. One can be the apostle of a church (2 Cor 8:23; Phil 2:25), but Paul is an apostle of Jesus Christ (Rom 1:1; 1 Cor 1:1; 2 Cor 1:1; Gal 1:1; Eph 1:1; 1 Tim 1:1; 2 Tim 1:1; Titus 1:1).

It is none other than **Messiah Jesus** who is the source of Paul's commission and authority as an apostle. Unlike other Pauline letters, what is at stake here is not Paul's authority as an apostle (e.g., Gal, 2 Cor), but the nature of the sending figure **Messiah Jesus** in light of the Colossian philosophy. I have rendered *Christos Iēsous* as **Messiah Jesus**, using "Messiah" rather than "Christ" for *Christos* in order to emphasize the Jewish and eschatological connotation of the designation for Paul (although I rec-

33

ognize that this was not necessarily evident to all readers).[1] While the Greek word *Christos* may be (or is on the way to becoming) a proper name, it has not lost all of its titular significance.[2] "Christ" is perhaps a cognomen like "Caesar" of "Gaius Julius Caesar." But just like "Caesar," "Christ" can also have a titular and regal meaning. We should not forget that *Christos* is often a Greek translation for the Hebrew *masiah* and the Aramaic *mesiha* from which we get "Messiah." A reverse order of "Jesus Messiah" or "Jesus Christ" is more common in Paul (e.g., 1:3) and underscores its titular nature especially when coordinate to "Lord," i.e., "Lord Jesus Christ." Indeed, Christ Jesus/Jesus Christ arguably evokes a titular sense of "Jesus the Messiah" and perhaps even an implied confession of "Jesus is the Messiah" as well. Such a title or confession conjures up an implied narrative about the life, death, and exaltation of Jesus. In other words, **Messiah Jesus** or **Jesus Messiah** is essentially an encoded reference to the *status* and *story* of Jesus of Nazareth as the king of Israel and exalted Lord of the world.[3]

Although Paul's apostolate is anchored in **Messiah Jesus**, it is also in accordance with **the will of God**, adding a theocentric dimension to Paul's apostolic office. His service rendered to Jesus is ultimately operative through divine empowerment, i.e., God working through Paul. God is working out his will, plan, and purpose through the Pauline mission. Paul is looped in a circle of authority between **Messiah Jesus** and **God**, as Dunn comments: "Paul as apostle of Christ Jesus, Jesus as Christ owned and authorized by God, and God as the one God of Israel through whose Messiah and apostle good news is extending to the nations."[4] Paul is not alone in his missionary endeavors. He has a cohort of coworkers and naturally makes mention of his cosender **Timothy [our] brother** (perhaps the scribe and coauthor of the epistle). Timothy, a disciple from Lystra (Acts 16:1–3), is a cosender in other correspondence (2 Cor 1:1; Phil 1:1; 1 Thess 1:1; 2 Thess 1:1; Phlm 1). Later in the epistle Paul will add mention of Tychicus as another **brother** who was quite likely the letter carrier accompanied by Onesimus (4:7–9).

---

1. A good justification for this strategy is provided by Blomberg 2003.

2. Cf. Wright 1986: 46–47; Barth and Blanke 1994: 137; Thompson 2005: 18.

3. According to Barth and Blanke (1994: 146), "The meaning of 'gospel' is pregnantly expressed in these first two verses of Col."

4. Dunn 1996: 47.

Paul does not address the letter to the "churches" in the designated region as he does elsewhere (e.g., Corinth [1 Cor 1:2; 2 Cor 1:1]; Galatia [Gal 1:1]; Thessalonica [1 Thess 1:1; 2 Thess 1:1]), yet this is hardly significant since he does not mention any particular "church" in the opening prescript of Romans, Philippians, or Ephesians either. For Paul, the fact that the gospel had spread to Colossae and the fact that they had been baptized into the Messiah is proof enough of the existence of an *ekklēsia* ("church") in Colossae. He describes them as **holy and faithful**. I have chosen to take *hagioi* ("saints" or "holy") adjectivally with **faithful**, which modifies **brothers and sisters** (on translating *adelphos* in this inclusive way see also NET, TNIV, NRSV, NLT).[5] The Colossians are, by reality and ideal, the holy and faithful people of God rooted in the Messiah. Holiness and fidelity describes their current state as those who are in Messiah, but it also designates the goal of their conduct as those who seek to live worthily of Messiah (see 1:10). The letter opening rounds up with a greeting of **grace and peace**. Paul has replaced the regular Greek *chairein* ("greeting") with *charis* ("grace," "favour," "generosity") and linked it characteristically to the Jewish concept of *shalom* ("peace"), understood as the absence of hostilities, but also well-being, wholeness, and prosperity. The apostle greets the Colossians with a blessing of divine favor and divine embrace.

---

5. Although in other letter prescripts *hagioi* is used substantively and appropriately translated as "saints" or "holy ones" (e.g., 1 Cor 1:2), Paul's only other use of *hagioi* in Colossians (3:12) is adjectival. See also Moule 1957: 45.

THANKSGIVING AND INTERCESSION:
The Prayer of Paul for the Colossians (1:3–14)

3 We always give thanks to the God and Father of our Lord Jesus *Christ* for you in prayer, 4 since we heard of your faithfulness in Messiah Jesus and the love which you have for all the saints, 5 because of the hope laid up for you in the heavenlies, which you first heard in the word of truth: the gospel. 6 This gospel has come to you just as in all the world it is bearing fruit and growing, just as among you from the day you heard and knew the grace of God in truth. 7 Just as you learned it from Epaphras our beloved fellow slave. He is a faithful servant of the Messiah on our behalf 8 and made known to us your love in the Spirit.

9 Because of this we also, from the very day we heard about you, have not ceased praying for you and petitioning God so that you might be filled in the knowledge of his will with complete wisdom and spiritual insight, 10 so as to walk worthily of the Lord and pleasing him in every way, bearing fruit in every good work and growing in the knowledge of God, 11 being strengthened with all power according to his glorious might for endurance and patience. With joy, 12 giving thanks to the Father who qualified you to share in the inheritance of the saints in the light. 13 He delivered us from the dominion of darkness and transferred us to the kingdom of the Son of his love, 14 in whom we have redemption, the forgiveness of sins.

Paul moves beyond his prescript into a rich prayer of thanksgiving and petition for the Colossians. Central to his prayer is the connection of the gospel to the Colossian assembly, their spiritual nourishment, the transformation of their minds, and the worthiness of their behavior before the Lord.

Hellenistic letters often began with a note of thanksgiving to the gods for certain persons or events. The inclusion of a thanksgiving section in personal communication carried over into Hellenistic Judaism, as evidenced by 2 Macc 1:10–13 where a letter from the Jews of Jerusalem to Jews in Egypt includes thanking God for his deliverance from a perilous military threat. While the form is clearly indebted to Hellenistic letter writing conventions, the content is very much of a Jewish and Christian character. Thanks is given to the **God and Father of our Lord Jesus *Christ***, which is indicative of the binitarian devotional life of the first Christians focused on Father and Son.[1] Jewish "monotheism" is assumed here, but it is redrawn in light of belief in the life, death, resurrection, exaltation, and co-enthronement of Jesus who is both **Lord** and **Messiah** (see Acts 2:36).[2]

The thanksgiving prayer is of a piece with the other Pauline thanksgiving petitions (Rom 1:8; 1 Cor 1:4–9; Phil 1:3–11; 1 Thess 1:2–4; 2 Thess 1:3; Phlm 4–7; 2 Tim 1:3–7). This one is certainly longer than normal and it is rivaled in length and poetic poignancy only by Eph 1:1–14. The prayer is to some degree a general plea for the Colossians' spiritual well-being, but specific elements do occur in the prayer as well. These elements are most apparent at the mention of Epaphras whose authority and influence in Colossae perhaps now hangs in the balance. The emphasis on knowledge and insight in the prayer are a direct counterclaim to the Colossian philosophy. The identification of the **saints in the light** as angels can be related to surfacing issues of angelic worship and deliverance from malevolent spiritual powers. These are matters that Paul will pick up again in the letter. The apostle signals early on, in the language of worship and adoration, that the Colossians already have everything that the local teachers are promising them, and they have it in the gospel of the Messiah.

1. Cf. Hurtado 2003: 151–53.
2. Cf. Hurtado 2003: 179–84.

PAUL'S THANKSGIVING FOR THE COLOSSIANS' PARTICIPATION IN THE GOSPEL (1:3–8)

Paul's prayer begins with the first person plural **We always give thanks** and includes his coworkers in Ephesus (or Rome) and co-sender Timothy (cf. 1 Thess 1:2; 2 Thess 1:3). In ancient letters thanksgiving does not merely display gratitude, but also gives the occasion for praise. In ancient letters thanks was ordinarily given to the deity for the well being of the recipient and here Paul offers his thanks to **the God and Father of our Lord Jesus *Christ*.**[3] The plural possessive pronoun **our** includes both the sender and recipients as those who belong to **Jesus *Christ*.** The two entities (God the Father and Lord Jesus) suggest that both are to be identified with the God of Israel who is "Lord God." The designation **Lord Jesus *Christ*** is ubiquitous in the NT. Jesus as Lord is accompanied by reference to "God and Father" in a number of places in Paul's letters.[4] Later in Col 3:17 Paul urges the Colossians to offer thanks to God through/in the Lord Jesus. In Phil 2:11 the exaltation of Jesus as Lord is bound up with the glory of the Father. What Jesus's lordship means is best spelled out by "he is Lord of all" (Acts 10:36).

The grounds for Paul's thanksgiving is expressed in the triadic formula of **faithfulness . . . love . . . hope.** The formula is common in Paul (Rom 5:1–5; Gal 5:5–6; 1 Thess 1:3; Eph 4:2–5) and in other Christian literature, suggesting that it was a shorthand Christian virtue list (Heb 6:10–12; 10:22–24; 1 Pet 1:3–8, 21–22; *Barn.* 1:4; 11:8).[5] Paul and his companions have received reports from Epaphras of the Colossians' **faithfulness in Messiah.** Although *pistis* could be translated as "faith," I find **faithfulness** to be the more likely given the literary context that focuses on action and attitudes rather than on assent to a *depositum cre-*

---

3. I have put "Christ" in italics because it is used as a proper name here. In addition, its textual integrity has some measure of doubt because (1) the word is not in B and little reason for scribal omission (other than error) can be given, and (2) nowhere else in Colossians is "Jesus Christ" found.

4. Cf. Rom 1:7; 15:6; 1 Cor 1:3; 8:6; 2 Cor 1:2–3; 11:31; Gal 1:3; Eph 1:2–3, 17; 5:20; 6:23; Phil 1:2; 2:11; 1 Thess 1:1–3; 3:11–13; 2 Thess 1:2; 2:16; 1 Tim 1:2; 2 Tim 1:2; Phlm 3.

5. Cf. Lightfoot (1879: 134): "Faith rests on the past; love works in the present; hope looks to the future"; Thompson (2005: 19): "The Christian virtues of 'faith' and 'love' are not only responses to but also effects of the grace and power of the gospel of Christ."

dendi or a body of teachings about Christ.[6] This faithfulness is expressed **in Messiah**, that is, within the sphere of Jesus's lordship, as opposed to rendering him simply the object of faith itself.[7] The Colossians are also known for their **love** for the **saints** which expresses a sense of affection and belonging to other Jesus-believers whom they have not yet met. The relationship of **hope** to the preceding virtues is difficult to gauge. The causal clause (*dia*) might suggest that **hope** is the basis of their **faithfulness** and **love**. Alternatively, the clause may relate back to the dominating verb above, **we always give thanks** (*eucharistoumen*), and provide a further reason for praise and gratitude to God.[8] The hope is described as **laid up for you in the heavenlies** and the word for **laid up** (*apokeimai*) can denote either something put away for safekeeping (e.g., Luke 19:20) or reserved as a reward (e.g., 2 Tim 4:8). Both senses are allowable although the emphasis should probably fall on the former as it is the sense of security and certainty (i.e., assurance) that is paramount. Later on Paul will refer to the return of the Messiah as the **hope of glory**, as the time when Jesus will finally be **manifested** (1:27; 3:4).[9] Even with the emphasis on present or realized eschatology (e.g., 2:11–13), there is no evacuation of an apocalyptic hope or a collapse into an entirely present eschatological experience. The point being pressed is that the Colossians' own hope is bound up with the Messiah as God's co-regent. He is now enthroned in the **heavenlies** and the hope centered on him is certain and unfailing. The purported governance of the angelic powers over daily life as stipulated by the philosophy may call precisely for the present reign of the Messiah to be emphasized.

The hope that centers on the exaltation of the Messiah was made known to the Colossians through **the word of truth: the gospel**. Here **gospel** stands in apposition to **word of truth**. This description is naturally contrasted with Paul's assessment of the teachings of the philoso-

---

6. It is my contention that *pistis* has the meaning of "faith" as doctrinal content in Col 1:23; 2:7, but it denotes "faithfulness" in Col 1:4; 2:5. I would add that any absolute bifurcation between "faith" and "faithfulness" is pointless, since Christian faithfulness will always require continued adherence and fidelity to a delivered body of teaching. See further Barth and Blanke 1994: 152–53; idem. 2000: 273–74; Thompson 2005: 19.

7. See Lightfoot 1879: 133; Moule 1957: 49; Lohse 1971: 16; O'Brien 1982: 11; Harris 1991: 16; Thompson 2005: 19; McL. Wilson 2005: 86; MacDonald 2008: 37.

8. Cf. Abbott 1897: 196.

9. BDAG 113.

phy, which are said to consist of empty deceit and human tradition (2:8). Moreover, much like the word of God in the Psalms (e.g., Ps 119:43), the word of the gospel is true and trustworthy. The epistle to the Colossians as a whole is "word" centered as evidenced by reference to the word of God, the word of Christ, and the word of evangelistic preaching (1:25; 3:16; 4:3). The Colossians are invited to see their own lives as part of the story of the gospel as viewed through their experience of deliverance and in their expression of faithfulness to the Messiah.

Paul then shifts his view to a wider horizon in the spread of the gospel in the worldwide theater. Paul says that **in all the world** the gospel is **bearing fruit and growing**. That is to say, the word of the gospel is being heard and garnering adherents across various political, ethnic, and territorial borders. The language here probably alludes to Gen 1:28 where Adam and Eve were to "Be fruitful and multiply and fill the earth." Taken up here, the progeny of Jesus, the new Adam, are doing just that, and obedience to God's gospel-word is the means by which the old world is colonized by the new humanity of the new creation (see 1:10).[10] We can also see here a possible allusion to Isa 27:6, which says, "In days to come Jacob shall take root, Israel shall blossom and put forth shoots and fill the whole world with fruit" (ESV). The great redemption of Israel that Isaiah predicted with its replanting of Israel produces an abundance of fruit that grows into the entire world. So too does the redemption in Messiah Jesus and the calling of the church to be Israel-for-the-sake-of-the-world bring forth a fruit basket of blessings that covers the earth.

The ideas here are made emphatic by the repetition of **just as** (*kathōs*). Just as the gospel came to the Colossians, so too has it come to others in the wider Greco-Roman world. Whereas biblical scholarship has tended to think of Christian communities as somewhat isolated and introspective entities, in actuality, the circulation of written materials and the travel itineraries of the early Christians suggest that they had a sense of being a worldwide movement and were very much in close and constant contact with one another.[11] It is reception and continued adherence to the gospel which will ensure that the Colossians remain in communion with a wider body of believers. It is their instruction from **Epaphras** that

10. Beale (2007: 846) regards Paul's usage here as "typological" as "the continued failure to fulfill the Genesis commission pointed to an eschatological humanity that would finally be obedient to the Genesis command."

11. Cf. Wright 1986: 73–74; Thompson 1998; Hvalvik 2005; Trebilco 2006.

connects them to this trans-provincial movement. Through Epaphras, the Colossians have **learned** the gospel, the life of faith in the Messiah, and no doubt news about other churches in Palestine, Syria, Asia Minor, Greece, and Italy too. Epaphras's status, and therefore his continuing influence in Colossae, is lauded by Paul when he calls Epaphras a **beloved fellow-slave** and **faithful servant**. Paul uses similar terms for other coworkers elsewhere (e.g., Tychicus in 4:7) and the place of Epaphras as a member in the Pauline circle is emphasized in the phrase **on our behalf**,[12] suggesting that Epaphras was Paul's representative in Colossae. He is the cipher through which mutual and reciprocal relations are established between Paul, his coworkers, and the Pauline churches on one side and the Colossian believers on the other. Epaphras then has a unique role as giving testimony to Paul's gospel in Colossae and also giving testimony about the Colossians' mutual affection for other assemblies of Jesus Christ. Thus, from a social perspective, Paul is very much interested in amicable and sustained relationships between himself and the Colossians, and to validate the ministry of Epaphras as well.

Paul's Petition for the Colossians to Anticipate Their Growth and Renewal in Messiah (1:9–14)

The second half of Paul's prayer shifts from thanksgiving to intercession. Paul's prayer, marked with urgency and emphasis (hence, **not ceased praying for you**), turns to matters of knowledge, wisdom, understanding, lifestyle, divine empowerment, and spiritual fruits among the Colossians. The prayer is not only Paul's, but is that of his companions too, as implied by the plural pronoun **we**. Paul twice mentions **knowledge** (*epignōsei*) which has led some to infer that Paul (or a post-Pauline author) is engaging Gnosticism. However, "knowledge" was not the essence of Gnosticism and all religions and philosophies have a form of intellectual content.[13] The object of Paul's **praying** and **petitioning** is for the Colossians to grasp the

---

12. Along with a number of ancient witnesses I have adopted the reading of "our behalf" as opposed to "your behalf" (P46 ℵ* B D* F G) since it is the more difficult reading and has the earliest textual support. See also Moule 1957: 27 n.1; Pokorný 1991: 44 n. 50; Wolter 1993: 56.

13. Cf. McL. Wilson (2005: 103): "The later development of the Gnostic Sophia myth is not directly relevant to the study of Colossians, but it is sometimes important to be aware of the final outcome."

source and content of true knowledge. This form of knowledge accords with God's **will** or purpose, it is **spiritual** as opposed to philosophical, and derives from a God-centered wisdom rather than a human derived tradition. That God grants understanding is axiomatic in Judaism (e.g., Dan 2:21; 9:22; 1QS 11:17–18; Wis 9:17; Sir 39:6–7), but Paul's conviction is that it is the Spirit of God as known through Christ who brings discernment to the things of God (see 1 Cor 2:6–16). What is more, the true test of religious learning is its ability to transform behavior, precisely what the philosophy lacks (see 2:23). Hence, Paul's prayer for the Colossians is that through apprehension of this knowledge they **walk worthily of the Lord and pleasing him in every way, bearing fruit in every good work**. This statement displays Paul's distinctive *halakah* or walk before God that endeavors to conform disciples to the pattern of the gospel.[14] The metaphor of a walk before God was important in Jewish piety (e.g., Exod 18:20; Deut 13:4–5; Ps 86:11) and in Paul's exhortations elsewhere (e.g., Gal 5:16; 2 Cor 5:7). The true test of knowledge is that it is noetically enriching, spiritually maturing, conforms to God's purpose, and results in patterns of behavior that are honoring of the Lord. The fruits of such knowledge speak for themselves: **endurance and patience.** The endurance motif is particularly important in light of what Paul will say in Col 1:23 about continuing securely in the faith and not shifting from the hope of the gospel. While God provides strength and power for the believer, he or she is still required to seek God's will and to honor God in order to persevere and endure in the faith contained in the gospel.

Paul proceeds to call the Colossians to be full of thankfulness towards God and accompanied with **joy**. The reason for this joy is that the **Father** has **qualified you to share in the inheritance of the saints in the light**. The word *hikanoō* means to make sufficient, adequate, or qualified (see 2 Cor 3:6). Ironically, whereas the Father has qualified them, the Colossians are giving ear to those who want to "disqualify" them (see 2:18). This is similar to the language of "justification" insofar as God has bestowed a special status on the Colossian believers that is complete, comprehensive, and requires no supplementary addition achieved through tertiary rituals. What the Father has qualified them for is more interesting. **Inheritance** has an obvious background in the Old Testament, and the land was Israel's inheritance (e.g., Deut 26:1–2; Josh 11:23; Ps 105:11). However, in the

14. See also Phil 1:27: "live your life in a manner worthy of the gospel of Christ."

New Testament **inheritance** (usually *klēronomia*) has a decidedly non-geographic meaning and is synonymous with salvation (Eph 1:14, 18), the future expression of the kingdom (Eph 5:5), eternal life (Heb 9:15; 11:8), heaven (1 Pet 1:4), and a heavenly reward (Col 3:24). In line with Col 3:24, this "inheritance" or "lot" (*klēros*) is probably to be identified with a transcendent reward associated with sharing in the **saints in the light**. This is an enigmatic phrase and some translations seek to remove the strangeness by adding "*kingdom of* light," which is not in the Greek text (NIV). The addition of "kingdom" is understandable given the reference to the "kingdom" of the Son in v. 14. If the **saints** are believers (see 1:4, 26) then the parallel in Ephesians is quite relevant and this refers to "his glorious inheritance among the saints" (Eph 1:18; cf. 5:5). Paul might be saying no more than that the Colossians have a part in the glorious inheritance of God's people in the heavenlies. But two things count in favor of an alternative proposal. First, **saints** or "holy ones" (*hagioi*) can also refer to angels (e.g., Zech 14:5; *1 En.* 1:9; *Pss. Sol.* 17:43; 1QS 11:7–8; cf. 1 Thess 3:13; 2 Thess 1:10). Second, **light** (*phōs*) is an odd qualification for "saints" unless it refers to their transcendent and glorious destiny (e.g., Rev 21:24). However, light is also associated with angels (Acts 12:7; 2 Cor 11:14; 1QS 3:20) and light is something that comes from heaven during visions and visitations (Acts 9:3; 22:6; 26:13; Tob 5:10). Given the debate about the worship of/with angels in Col 2:18, Paul might be suggesting that believers have been qualified to inherit the rights and privileges normally given to angelic beings.[15]

The Lord is then defined as the one **who delivered us from the dominion of darkness and transferred us to the kingdom of the Son of his love**. This short but tightly packed expression exhibits a number of key Pauline themes. First, there is an apocalyptic orientation as believers have been rescued from malevolent spiritual forces bound up with the current age (see Gal 1:4; Col 2:15). Second, we have here the language of wide scale transportation as the word **transferred** (*methistēmi*) can be used in regards to the transplantation of entire peoples (Josephus *Ant.* 9.235). God has picked up his people and transplanted them into a whole new territory. Paul frames salvation in terms reminiscent of the exodus where believers experience a new exodus and a new redemption by entering into

15. Cf. Lohse 1971: 35; Martin 1973: 54; Sappington 1991: 199; MacDonald 2008: 50; contra Harris 1991: 34; Barth and Blanke 1994: 186; Dunn 1996: 76–77; Witherington 2007: 125 n. 22.

the imperishable inheritance of God (see common language with Exod 6:6; 14:30; Deut 13:5; Judg 6:9 [LXX]).[16] There might be a more specific allusion to Isaiah's appropriation of the exodus theme given the picture of Israel being restored from "darkness" to "light" in Isa 9:1–2, 42:6–7, 16, 58:10, 60:1–3.[17] Third, while there is a paucity of references to **king-dom** in Paul, it is no less significant.[18] For Paul, the kingdom of God is something that is principally future (reward, judgment, consummation), but is already affecting the present.[19] Indeed, the entire experience of salvation can be defined as "kingdom" in some respects. Paul here places kingdom in proximity to the **Son**, underscoring the unique relation that Jesus has to the Father and his singular role in inaugurating and executing the Father's kingdom (also with obvious echoes of a messianic reading of 2 Sam 7:13–17 and Ps 2:7).[20] The Son is also the sphere of the Father's saving activity and it is in him that believers apprehend **redemption, the forgiveness of sins**. The concept of redemption for Greco-Roman persons was known through the manumission of slaves. Redemption meant release by the payment of a price. Elsewhere in his letters Paul states how that price was paid (e.g., Rom 3:24; Eph 1:7; 1 Cor 6:20; 1 Tim 2:6; Titus 2:14).[21] Specifically, redemption is here correlated with the **forgiveness of sins**. Many of Paul's metaphors for salvation overlap. For instance, forgiveness is linked to justification (Acts 13:38–39; Rom 4:7–8) and redemption (Col 1:14; Eph 1:7). Elsewhere in the New Testament forgiveness is related to sacrifice (Heb 9:22; 10:18) and cleansing (1 John 1:9). Concepts of redemption and forgiveness go naturally together since both are concerned

---

16. Cf. Lohse 1971: 37; Wright 1986: 60–63; Wall 1993: 58–61; Dunn 1996: 77, 80; MacDonald 2008: 51.

17. Cf. Barth and Blanke 1994: 188, 190–93; Beale 2007: 849.

18. Cf. Rom 14:17; 1 Cor 4:20; 6:9–10; 15:24, 50; Gal 5:21; Eph 5:5; Col 4:11; 1 Thess 2:12; 2 Thess 1:5; 2 Tim 4:1; 4:18; and Acts 14:22; 19:8; 20:25; 28:23, 31. (See Wenham 1995: 71–80.)

19. Cf. Wright (1986: 62): "On the basis of 1 Corinthians 15:23–28 we may infer . . . that Paul conceived of the establishment of this kingdom as a two-stage process. First there is 'the kingdom of Christ,' which begins with Christ's resurrection and exaltation and continues until all enemies are subdued. Then there comes the final kingdom of God, the restoration of all things."

20. Cf. Wolter 1993: 67.

21. Of course Paul can also mention "redemption" without mentioning the mechanism by which it occurs (Rom 8:23; 1 Cor 1:30; Gal 3:13; Eph 1:14). On redemption imagery in Paul, see Williams 1999: 122–24; Bird 2008a: 106–8.

with release. In the case of **forgiveness**, the word *aphesis* denotes ideas of liberation, release, pardon, or cancellation of obligation.

Fusing the Horizons: The Global Church

One of the many challenges that this text presents for the new covenant community is that it urges us to see ourselves as an international body of believers. The gospel has come to us, just as it came to others elsewhere in the world. The gospel is spreading and bearing fruit globally, just as it is among us. Thus, we should see ourselves as a small part of the wider global church made up of the multi-racial and multi-cultural people of God. This is all the more significant in the current global context where Christianity is declining (numerically and spiritually) in Europe and North America, but rising in Africa, Asia, and South America. Indeed, in some denominational contexts like Anglicanism, it is leaders in Africa who are championing the cause of the gospel over and against the liberalizing tendencies of the Western church. This global perspective on Christianity must surely shape our doctrine of the church, practice of mission, and views of culture.

What begs for transformation in many cases is our ecclesiology. Why is the church so diverse, and is this a good thing? After all, diversity breeds difference, debate, and even division. Would not a uniform, homogenous, almost clone-like church be better for unity? Yet the body of Christ has an indelible and irreducible plurality built into it. The church is one body with many parts complete with a unity in diversity. Experiencing the power of forgiveness and being made part of the renewed Israel is a saving event that crosses racial, geographical, and cultural boundaries. Christians have a shared identity in Jesus Christ, they are part of a renewed Adamic race, they have accepted the call to come into Abraham's family of the faithful, they are forgiven of their wicked and godless ways, and they seek to cultivate the virtues of faith, hope, and love as well. That which unites them is infinitely stronger than anything that might divide them from one another. For me this imagery of the multi-national church was powerfully revealed when I visited a church where the minister arranged a video clip about all the people in his congregation of different nationalities. Each congregant of foreign background spoke of what faith in Christ meant for them given their background and heritage. It was a medium sized rural church, but they still had more than sixteen different nations represented in their parish. The climax of the event was when they brought out the sixteen flags of each nation represented in the congregation. No flag was raised above the others, no flags were bowed before another one, but at the end of the service all the flags were laid at the foot of a cross.

In addition, an ethnically diverse church has some key advantages for missions. I have been made aware of how Christians from Latin America have been successfully reaching out to Muslims in Europe. The advantage that Latin Americans have is that their skin colour is similar to Arabs and Asians, they are Christian but not white Anglo-Saxons, there is no history of conflict between the Middle East and South America, both groups hail from developing countries with generally strong family units and relatively conservative moral values, and both groups are resident aliens in the new Europe. It is precisely the culture and nationality of these Latin American missionaries that makes them far more able to reach out to Muslims in Europe where many simply cannot penetrate effectively. By divine providence, then, there is a great diversity to the body of Christ that enables the mission of God to be accomplished through the culturally diverse, multi-ethnic, and global church of Jesus Christ.

THE SUPREMACY OF MESSIAH IN CREATION AND RECONCILIATION:
The Christ Hymn (1:15–20)

The most frequently cited and studied part of Colossians is the Christ Hymn of 1:15–20. Here (together with Phil 2:4–11; John 1:1–18; and Heb 1:1–4) we have one of the most sublime and profound descriptions of the person and work of Jesus Christ in the New Testament. The scholarship on this short piece of text is immense and nearly everything about the passage is disputed.[1]

[15] He is the image of the invisible God
> the firstborn of all of creation
>> [16] because in him were created
>>> all things in the heavens and upon the earth
>>> the visible and the invisible
>>> whether thrones or lords or rulers or authorities
>> all things were created through him and for him.

[17] And he is before all things
> and all things are sustained in him.

[18] And he is the head
> of the body, the church.

He is the beginning
> the firstborn from the dead in order that in all things he might have
>> preeminence
>>> [19] because in him [God] was pleased to have all his fullness dwell
>>> [20] and through him to reconcile to himself all things
>>>> by making peace through the blood of his cross through him
>>>> whether upon the earth or in the heavens

---

1. See Bruce 1984b; Wright 1991: 99–119; Barclay 1997: 58–68; C. Stettler 2000; Kooten 2003; McL. Wilson 2005: 122–59; Pizzuto 2006; Smith 2006: 146–72; Gordley 2007.

This passage is probably a Christian hymn or poem about Jesus Christ. The use of relative clauses in verses 15 and 18 is indicative of other confessional and hymnic materials in the New Testament (e.g., Rom 4:25; Phil 2:6; 1 Tim 3:16; Heb 1:3; 1 Pet 2:21–24). Paul is probably using some traditional material given the unique vocabulary, the liturgical feel, and the near intrusion of the text upon the immediate literary context. However, it is almost impossible to gauge what the original "poem" was and what Paul has added, subtracted, or rearranged.[2]

The religious-historical background of this pre-Pauline poem is disputed in scholarship (some even suggest that it is a pre-Christian text that has been taken up by Christians). First, there have been proposals that the background to the poem lies in a gnostic redeemer myth where an archetypal human comes to redeem the human race from corruption and the mortal condition.[3] This is improbable because: (1) There is no extant pre-Christian evidence of a gnostic redeemer who entered into the world of darkness in order to redeem the sons of light by becoming the "redeemed Redeemer." There was then no gnostic redeemer myth that was waiting in the wings to be taken up, Christianized, and applied to Jesus. This "redeemed Redeemer" is himself a "myth" of mid-twentieth-century German scholarship. (2) It is not a "supra-historical" perspective or elements of a "metaphysical drama" that typified Gnosticism, rather, it was an "anti-cosmic dualism" that drove a wedge between the good god of salvation and the malevolent god of creation that lay at the core of Gnosticism. (3) A gnostic hymn would be unlikely to trace creation and reconciliation to the same divine being. (4) It is impossible to excise all Christian traits from the poem as "firstborn" and "reconcile" are near technical Christian terms here.

Second, others have argued that it reflects mediator figures from Hellenistic Judaism, most notably personifications of Wisdom extant in Jewish wisdom literature (e.g., Sirach and Wisdom of Solomon) and the *Logos* from Philo.[4] The problem is that while the parallels with Wisdom are numerous they are often oblique. For example, Wisdom is often regarded as a created entity (Prov 8:22–23; Sir 1:4, 9), whereas in the poem

2. If there is anything that might be distinctly Pauline here it is probably the reference to the church as the "body" and the "blood of his cross."

3. Cf. Käsemann 1964.

4. Cf. Lightfoot 1879: 143–44; Lohse 1971: 46–47; Martin 1973: 58; Barclay 1997: 66–67; Dunn 1998: 269, 275–77; Lincoln 2000: 605; Witherington 2007: 130–33.

Jesus is closer to the role of creator and is not part of the created order. What is more, there is no known reference to the world being created for Wisdom.[5]

Third, others argue that the poem represents a christological interpretation of Genesis 1 and the language of "image" and "beginning" finds suitable parallels there.[6] C. F. Burney proposes that the poem understands the figure of Wisdom in Prov 8:22 in light of Gen 1:1.[7] He makes much of the Hebrew compound word *bereshith* ("in the beginning") in highlighting the instrument of divine agency in creation. Overall, I find this third option the most likely. The poem is evidently rooted in the Jewish framework of monotheism, creation, and intermediaries with clear echoes of Gen 1:1, 26–27. As such, Jesus is the "image" of the new eschatological humanity and the "beginning" of the new creation. Though I admit that links with wisdom traditions are simply too plain to ignore.[8] I suggest, then, that it is precisely because Jewish wisdom theology was so indebted to Jewish views of creation that links between Col 1:15–20 and Sirach, Proverbs, Philo, and Wisdom of Solomon can be found.[9] The most analogous text, however, is probably 1 Cor 8:6. Taken together, 1 Cor 8:6 and Col 1:15–20 provide an affirmation of a Jewish creation scheme, Jewish monotheism, and God's action through intermediaries. Yet this well-

5. See the thorough critique in Fee 2007: 317–25.

6. Cf. Burney 1925; Davies 1955: 150–52; Moule 1957: 62; Wright 1986: 66–68; 1991: 99–119; Fee 2007: 299–300.

7. Burney 1925: 173–75; cf. Wright 1991: 111–12.

8. (1) In Gen 1:1 LXX, *archē* ("beginning") is a translation of the Hebrew *reshith* (Col 1:18); (2) *reshith* is a polysemous word and can mean "beginning," "first-born," "chief," and "head" (Col 1:15, 18); (3) the preposition *be* ("in, with, by") in *bereshith* might correspond to the prepositional clauses "in him," "through him," and "for him" (= Col 1:16–17, 19–20); (4) in the LXX *eikōn* ("image") occurs in Gen 1:26–27 for Adam (Col 1:15); (5) in terms of links with Jewish Hellenistic wisdom traditions we should note that Wisdom is among the first things created in the "beginning" (Prov 8:22–23; cf. Sir 1:4, 9; 24:9), Wisdom is the "image" of Gods goodness (Wis 7:26), elsewhere "all things were made in wisdom" (Ps 103:24 LXX; cf. Wis 8:5; 9:1–2; Prov 3:19; Philo *Det.* 54), Philo calls Wisdom the "beginning and image and sight of God" (*Leg.* 1.43) and the Logos is "the beginning and name of God, and the Word, and man according to God's image, and he who sees Israel" (*Conf.* 146). According to Smith (2006: 161), "It can be concluded that *eikōn tou theou* is reflective of a Jewish tradition of an anthropomorphous hypostatic representation of God."

9. For a combination of both Old Testament imagery and Jewish Hellenistic wisdom traditions see Dahl 1964: 434; O'Brien 1982: 38–40, 43–44, 61–62. Beale (2007: 855) also shows that wisdom and adamic traditions are not mutually exclusive.

known paradigm is radically redrawn around a particular view of Israel's Messiah as participating in the divine acts of creation and redemption.

The structure is particularly hard to determine, mainly because the wording is asymmetrical, and the shift from vv. 12–14 to vv. 15–20 is hardly abrupt. The most likely option appears to be that the poem is framed in two major strophes (vv. 15–16; 18b–20) both beginning with a relative clause and with two lines (vv. 17–18a) sandwiched in the middle functioning as an abridgment.[10] In my opinion, the coherence and unity of the poem is based around certain key motifs in both strophes that are activated by certain words.

He is . . .	Divine Personhood: The identity of Jesus in relation to God.
Firstborn	Divine Preeminence: The supremacy of Jesus over creation and new creation.
Because	Divine Perspective: An explanation of how Jesus relates to the prerogatives and presence of God.
In him	Divine Agency: What purposes God works out through the Son.
Whether . . .	Divine Authority: Signals the extent of the Son's reign over creation and salvation.

In terms of a rhetorical function, this passage operates much like a *propositio*, which sets forth the central thesis of the epistle.[11] It also has some affinities with Asiatic rhetoric, which tended to be far more ornamented, flowery, and even pompous at times. This rich tapestry of highly poetic and poignant christological imagery is set forth in order to

10. Cf. Martin 1973: 55–56; Lincoln 2000: 602–3; McL. Wilson 2005: 126–27, although I remain unsure about making vv. 17–18a a "strophe" of its own.

11. According to MacDonald (2008: 67) the principle themes of Colossians are announced in this hymn, including: Christ's preeminence as foundation for the arguments against the "philosophers," the reigning Christ prepares the way for the proclamation that believers have been raised and co-enthroned with Christ, and body symbolism which is central to the cosmic and social integration of Colossians. For Lohse (1971: 178) this section provides the *leitmotif* that runs throughout the letter and is the basis for all subsequent christological reflection. Barth and Blanke (1994: 194) say of Col 1:15–20, "These thoughts form the basis for the principal affirmation of Col." As such I disagree with Witherington (2007: 128) who sees it as part of the *narratio*, and Lincoln (2000: 557) who identifies it within the *exordium*.

persuade the Colossians of the sufficiency and supremacy of the Messiah over all things in creation and make him the exclusive agent of salvation. Socially the poem functions here to reinforce the ideological boundaries between the "faith" of the Pauline churches and the deviance of the philosophy that devalues the place of Christ in the cosmological order.[12] Indeed, Paul's inclusion of this poem is intended as a polemic primarily against a particular cosmology upon which the teachers' aberrant Christology is based. The issue is far more than, "Is Jesus God or is he only quasi-divine?" More appropriately, it asks what place Jesus occupies in the cosmological order in relation to the one God of Israel, and to various spiritual entities with varying degrees of power and authority as well.[13] The poem is deployed here in aid of creating a symbolic universe that is defined chiefly by a "christological monotheism" over and against the angelology of the philosophy.[14] All this through a short piece of primitive Christian hymnody!

THE SUPREMACY OF THE MESSIAH IN CREATION (1:15–16)

The content in vv. 12–14 might represent a piece of traditional material like a baptismal liturgy, but it is impossible to tell its origins and function.[15] Nonetheless, Paul proceeds to include some traditional material in vv. 15–20. Verses 15–17 focus specifically on the Messiah's relation to creation. Paul begins with **He is the image of the invisible God. Image** (*eikōn*) conveys the sense of that which has the same form as something else.[16] Jesus has the same form or reflection as God, which is reminiscent of Phil 2:6, where Jesus was in the "form of God" prior to his incarna-

12. Cf. Wright 1991: 118.

13. According to Dunn (1996: 97), Paul moves from a "cosmology of creation to a cosmology of reconciliation."

14. On a symbolic universe in Colossians see MacDonald 2008: 68–70; Talbert 2007: 192–93.

15. On 1:12–14 as traditional material see Cannon 1983: 12–19. He writes: "While the traditional character of 1:12–14 cannot be proved with certainty, the evidence points to the probability of such a conclusion. The opening participle *eucharistountes* points to the confessional character of these verses. The change of pronouns and the style and language strongly suggest that the writer drew on an outside source. And finally, the manner in which the concepts related to the Exodus motif are presented intimate the sacrament of baptism as the source of the homology" (19).

16. BDAG 282.

tion; Heb 1:3, where Jesus is the "radiance" and "exact replica" of God's glory and being; and obviously 2 Cor. 4:4, where the glorious Christ is the "image of God." The key ideas are representation and manifestation.[17] The mention of **image** also relates back to Gen 1:26–27 where Adam and Eve were the bearers of the divine image. What the *imago Dei* (image of God) exactly is remains disputed by theologians. Since kings in the ancient Near East were supposed to be the image or shadow of God, it may mean no more than that humanity is royal in God's eyes.[18] That accords with the role given to humanity as rulers over creation in Gen 1:26–30 and the focus of the poem on Jesus's sovereignty. As the image of God, then, Jesus is the new eschatological Adam of God's renewed creation, which corresponds once more with what Paul says elsewhere in 1 Cor 15:45, 47, where Christ, by virtue of his resurrection, is the "last Adam" and "second man." The image is related to the **invisible God**. That God was invisible (i.e., beyond the realm of human perception) was axiomatic in Jewish thought and reaffirmed in the New Testament (e.g., Rom 1:20; 1 Tim 1:17; Heb 11:27). Indeed, as the image of God, Jesus makes the invisible visible for all to behold, underscoring the revelatory function of his imaging of God.[19] In sum, as the **image of the invisible God**, Jesus is: (1) of the same likeness or form of God; (2) the beginning of the new eschatological humanity,;and (3) the one who reveals God to human beings in his very person.

Paul then adds that Jesus is the **firstborn of all of creation. Firstborn** literally means "eldest child" (e.g., Gen 25:25 LXX; Luke 2:7; Heb 11:28). In a Greco-Roman household the firstborn was the designated heir of the estate, while in the Old Testament the firstborn son had special privileges of inheritance (Deut 21:15–17) and was dedicated to God (e.g., Exod 22:29; Num 3:12–13; 8:17–18). We should note also that Israel is called God's "firstborn son" (Exod 4:22; Jer 31:9; *4 Ezra* 6:58; *Pss. Sol.* 18:4; Philo *Fug.* 208) and Israel's king is likewise referred to as the "firstborn" and the "highest of the kings of the earth" (Ps 89:27). The word **firstborn** (*prōtotokos*) has also been a playground for ancient and modern theologians in light of controversies about the nature of Christ (especially

---

17. Lightfoot 1879: 145–46.

18. Cf. *NDIEC* 9:15, which mentions a papyrus ca. 221–25 BCE that refers to a king who is said to be "the living image of God."

19. Cf. Martin (1973: 57): "The description is revelatory, more than ontological."

the Arian controversy of the fourth century).[20] Does **firstborn** imply that Jesus is merely the most supreme created being? Hardly! The main point is surely Jesus's function in bringing creation into being and his sovereignty over the entire created order. That authority encompasses the material and immaterial realms, the earthly and heavenly spheres, human and angelic creatures.[21] Moreover, if Paul had wanted to suggest that Jesus was the first of God's creatures to be formed he would have used the adjective *prōtoktistos* ("created first") or the noun *prōtoplastos* ("first made"). The words for "firstborn" and "first-fruits" are ascribed to Jesus in the New Testament where they carry connotations of priority since Jesus is the firstborn of a new humanity which is to be glorified as its exalted Lord is glorified (Rom 8:29; 1 Cor 15:20, 23; Rev 1:5 and Col 1:18).[22] In Hebrews, "firstborn" implies a special status and higher rank over and above others (e.g. Heb 1:6). As the **firstborn** Jesus is: (1) God's appointed ruler over all of creation with priority in time and primacy in rank; (2) Israel's Messiah; and (3) a Son of God like Adam and Israel.

A rationale for these statements is given in a causal clause **because in him were created all things**, wherein **all things** encompasses every imaginable sphere including **heavens** and **earth,** things **visible** and **invisible.** The element of divine agency is repeated again when it is stated that all things were created **through him** as well. This underscores the notion of God the Father creating the world through his preexistent Son. In many ways, the Son appropriates the role normally attributed to the Spirit in the creation of the cosmos. What is unparalleled, christologically speaking, is that Paul says that the universe came into being **for him**.[23] It is hard to emphasize what a striking remark this is as it makes creation subordinate to Jesus the Messiah. This could mean that the universe came into existence for his benefit, but more likely it means that the universe exists in order to be his designated domain of authority. It is an authority

20. Cf. Lightfoot 1879: 148–50; Gorday 2000: 12–14.

21. Cf. H. Balz (*EDNT* 3:190–91) who sees "firstborn" as not just a "matter of purely temporal priority of the pre-existence Christ, but rather of a superiority of essence."

22. BDAG 894.

23. Cf. Martin (1973: 58): "No Jewish thinker ever rose to these heights in daring to predict that wisdom was the ultimate goal of creation"; and Lightfoot (1879: 155): "This expression has no parallel, and could have none, in the Alexandrian phraseology and doctrine." I think the closest analogy to this text is *4 Ezra* 6:53–59, which says that the world was created for "Israel," and the *Shepherd of Hermas* 8:1, which says that the world was created for the "church."

that rivals and exceeds **thrones or lords or rulers or authorities**.[24] These most likely refer to hostile angelic powers associated with the bondage of the present age that hold parts of the world in the sway of their dark grip (see Rom 8:38; 1 Cor 8:5. Eph 1:21; 6:12).[25] Later Paul will say quite dramatically that Jesus is their conqueror and champion (2:15).

THE BODY OF THE UNIVERSE AND THE BODY OF THE MESSIAH (1:17–18a)

The following verses inject, or perhaps even interrupt, the flow of the poem with some brief remarks about Jesus's priority to creation, his preservation of creation, and also of his authority over the church. Jesus is not the first of the created things but he is **before all things**, which lucidly ascribes to him preexistence. In another striking christological remark, Paul says that **all things are sustained in him**, which means that Christ is the reason why there is a *cosmos* instead of *chaos*.[26] This role is similar to that of the *Logos* in Stoic philosophy where the *Logos* is the captain or pilot of the universe. While the authority of Jesus is cosmic in scope, it is no less ecclesial. Even as the cosmic lord, Jesus remains the **head of the body, the church**. References to the church as the **body** are common in Paul[27] and the metaphor was well known in antiquity and could even be applied to the universe (e.g., Plato *Tim.* 28B).[28] Jesus is supreme over both such bodies.[29] As the "body of Messiah" the church is the physical

24. Arnold (1996: 254) points out that the *archai* ("rulers") and *exousiai* ("authorities") are part of the Jewish vocabulary for angelic beings, but are not common in Hellenism for gods, spirits, demons, or mediatory beings.

25. Cf. Gnilka 1980: 127; Arnold 1996: 253. Philo (*Gig.* 6), commenting on Gen 6:2, says, "Those beings, whom other philosophers call demons, Moses usually calls angels; and they are souls hovering in the air" (trans. Yonge).

26. Lightfoot 1879: 156.

27. Cf. 1 Cor 10:16–17; 12:12, 27; Rom 12:5; and more parallels in Eph 1:22–23; 4:15.

28. Cf. van Koonten 2003: 17–30, who supposes that a Stoic and Middle Platonist conception of the universe as a body stands behind 1:17, 2:9–10, 17, 19. At this point, the hymn is Stoic to the extent that it is concerned with the stability and coherence of the universe in the sense of what holds it together (2003: 19–20). But this section lacks the view of the cosmos as animated by the divine world-soul; instead, it is controlled by the head who is clearly the Messiah (Bruce 1984b: 105).

29. The metaphor of "body" could also be applied to the Roman people (Livy *Hist.* 2.32.9–12; Epictetus *Disc.* 2.10.4–5). We have an implied contrast between two bodies:

representation of Jesus upon the earth. The church (*ekklēsia*) here means the universal church. Jesus is the **head** of the church, not in the sense of its source, but as its titular head and leader. While the poem has a high Christology, it also has a high ecclesiology, as the one who is the creator of the cosmos is also the head of the church. However disjoined these verses initially appear to be, they subtly shift the subject matter from creation (all things are sustained in him) to reconciliation (the church as the body of people reconciled to God) and so assist in the progression of the poem to the next subject matter.

THE SUPREMACY OF THE MESSIAH IN RECONCILIATION (1:18b–20)

The next strophe of the poem begins with another relative clause, and two things stand out in juxtaposition here, viz., that Jesus is the **beginning** and **the firstborn from the dead**. The mention of **beginning** is a fairly obvious echo of Gen 1:1: "In the beginning . . ." As we saw earlier the word **firstborn** in the New Testament is used largely to denote Jesus as the prototype and provision for God's renewed humanity. The Jewish hope of resurrection, though not held uniformly by all devout Jews in the first century, looked ahead to the day when God would renew and recreate the entire world and return it to a period of Edenic goodness. Salvation is not escape from the created world through the release of an immortal soul encased in a body (as in Greek philosophy) or the liberation of the divine spark from its fleshly chrysalis (as in Gnosticism), rather salvation consists of the redemption of our bodies to live and abide in God's new world (see Rom 8:23). That new creation has kicked off, proleptically and quite unexpectedly, in the resurrection of Jesus. The resurrection of Jesus is also significant christologically because he is raised and exalted by God in order to rule beside God. It is hardly surprising then that New Testament references to Jesus as the firstborn or firstfruits of the general resurrection are bound up with the reign of God over the nations and the created order (see especially Rev 1:5–7 and 1 Cor 15:20–25).

Paul provides two reasons why God has purposed to launch this new creation through his Son and what singularly suited him for this redemptive role. First, God's plan was that in all things Jesus would have **preeminence**; analogous words are "supremacy" (NIV, NJB) or "first

---

one headed by Caesar and the other headed by Jesus.

place" (NRSV, NASB, NET).[30] Here we are talking about far more than being a very important person. We are talking about authority, honor, and power rolled into one. The most analogous background I can think of is the Roman emperor Augustus who claimed to exceed everyone in *auctoritas*, that is, a combination of power and prestige. The Augustan age created a pyramid of power and hierarchy that put him inviolably at the top. Indicative of this is that Augustus held the proconsulship of Rome well beyond the normal limitations of service; he was invested with the power of the tribunate with right of veto over the senate; he was the *princeps* or chief citizen of the government; he had direct military command of over three quarters of the Roman legions, the power of intervention in imperial provinces; and he was given titles like *pontifex maximus*, or "high priest" of the empire, and *Imperator Caesar divi filius*, "emperor and son of a god." The implied rhetoric in this poem is that as the preeminent one Jesus is the real *auctoritas* over and against the pretentious claims of earthly rulers to be sovereign and divine. This becomes all the more powerful if we remember that Paul is imprisoned, in Rome or Ephesus, during the reign of Emperor Nero when writing this. Roman emperors, at death or even while alive, could be lauded as a god, a son of god, or be numbered among a series of deities in a cosmic, cyclic order.[31] Political potentates and heavenly powers were intertwined in antiquity (e.g., Isa 14:4–27). But Caesar was at best a twisted parody of the real Lord of the world and at worst a malevolent tyrant who created "empire" and "peace" through the application of violence. The Pictish King Calgacus is portrayed as saying: "These plunderers of the world having taken all the land, now claim the seas, so that even if we fly to the sea there is no safety from them. They kill and slay, and take what is not theirs, and call it Empire. They make a desert and call it Peace."[32] The Jesus of Colossians brooks no rivals, be they the malevolent powers of the cosmos or brutal dictators in a foreign land. A second thought is proffered by Paul: Jesus has unique qualification to be the agent of reconciliation. Paul says that **in him [God] was pleased to have all his fullness dwell**. The subject for the verb **pleased** (*eudokeō*) is missing, but the implied subject is probably God (or perhaps a periphrasis: "God in all his fullness"). God was

---

30. The word *prōteuōn* might even be an honorific title. See *NDIEC* 2:96; and W. Michaelis, *TDNT* 6:881–82.

31. Maier 2005: 339.

32. Tacitus *Agr.* 30.

pleased to have **all his fullness** inhabit the Messiah. The word for **fullness** (*plērōma*) was a near technical term in Valentinian Gnosticism for the totality of intermediaries or emanations radiating from the supreme God. There may be an implied critique here of something from Hellenistic philosophy that eventually became part of a gnostic cosmological framework and might even be part of the Colossian philosophy,[33] but the main point is surely christological: the fullness of God—God's word, wisdom, glory, Spirit, and power—dwells in the Messiah.

In much the same way that this poem attributes to Jesus agency in creation, so now he is regarded as God's agent in reconciliation. Paul says that **through him** or by the activity of the Messiah, God was able to **reconcile to himself all things**. The word **reconcile** (*katalassō*) means to exchange hostility for a friendly relationship.[34] This implies a prior state of alienation and hostility between Creator and the creation which has now been restored (see Col 1:12; 2:15). Here we find that the offended party, God, takes the initiative in reconciliation in order to remove the hostility between himself and his creation. Furthermore, the object of reconciliation is not merely human beings, but **all things**, which gives reconciliation a cosmic scope as Paul says in 2 Cor 5:19: "God was in Christ reconciling *the world* to himself."[35] As Lohse comments, the "universe has been reconciled in that heaven and earth have been brought back into their divinely created and determined order . . . the universe is again under its head and . . . cosmic peace has returned."[36] The mechanism of reconciliation and thus **peace** is through the **blood of his cross**, and Paul elsewhere refers to the blood of Jesus's death with its particular atoning function in securing forgiveness, redemption, and justification (e.g., Rom 3:24–25; 4:7; 5:9). Just as things in the **heavens** and the **earth** were created in him, so now are all things in the same realms are reconciled to God through the blood of the cross.

---

33. Against reading second century Gnostic systems into this first century text see Lohse 1971: 57; Dunn 1996: 86 n. 8; McL. Wilson 2005: 153–54, 158–59; Lightfoot 1879: 158–59; contrasted with Baur 2003 [1873–75]: 2:9–12; Käsemann 1964: 158–59.

34. BDAG 521.

35. Cf. Bird 2008a: 104–6.

36. Lohse 1971: 59.

Fusing the Horizons: Christological Assertions

One could write, teach, preach, or discuss this text for hours and still only scratch the surface of its theological depth. We are presented with a theological kaleidoscope that blends cosmology, Christology, and soteriology in the one hit. In a sense, we could say that a major purpose of the poem is to praise Jesus Christ and to correct aberrant and competing portraits of his person and work. But it is far more than that, as Dunn colorfully writes:

> The vision is vast. The claim is mind-blowing. It says much for the faith of these first Christians that they should see in Christ's death and resurrection quite literally the key to resolving the disharmonies of nature and the inhumanities of humankind, that the character of God's creation and God's concern for the universe in its fullest expression could be so caught and encapsulated for them in the cross of Christ . . . In some ways still more striking is the implied vision of the church as the focus and means towards this cosmic reconciliation—the community in which that reconciliation has already taken place (or begun to take place) and whose responsibility it is to live out . . . as well as to proclaim its secret (cf. 4:2–6).[37]

The mileage one gets from this poem is not merely to make sure Christians believe the right stuff about Jesus, but to see Jesus and ourselves as part of the story of creation and reconciliation. The story of the church and of individual Christians themselves is written up in a narrative of a world made good, gone wrong, and being put right. It is part of a narrative tapestry related to the promises made to Abraham coming true at last in the cosmopolitan people belonging to Israel's Messiah. It encompasses human rebellion and divine reconciliation. It is a drama of despots and tyrants, spiritual and human (they were not always distinguished in the Bible),[38] being defeated through the blood of the cross.

There is no shirking away from the obvious christological assertions made here. The devotion of Christians is not offered to a cultic figure, but to the Lord through whom and for whom the world was made. It is stupendous that the

37. Dunn 1996: 146.

38. Cf. e.g. Luke 20:20; 2 Pet 2:10; Jude 8; and discussion in Thompson 2005: 34–39; Barth and Blanke 1994: 201–3.

Nazarene who had been executed only thirty years earlier was now heralded and identified with the God of creation and reconciliation.[39] There is no room for idolatry or pluralism. Jesus does not accept rivals and his supremacy has no limits. To quote Abraham Kuyper, there is nothing in the universe of which Jesus cannot say, "mine!" For members of the new covenant community, that means ordering their lives according to the teachings, symbols, story, mission, and purpose of their sovereign Lord. It means summoning an unbelieving world to faith and repentance in the one who commands their obedience and achieves their salvation. It means declaring to agents of evil and structures of injustice that people and their love for power will always succumb to the power of God's love in Messiah. Thus, the body of Christ can engage those structures and institutions that create war, poverty, and injustice. For instance, Christian organizations like the International Justice Mission attempt to secure justice for victims of slavery, sexual exploitation, and other forms of violent oppression. The Jesus who is proclaimed by the global church as Lord and Redeemer brings good news to the poor and oppressed. The Messiah will bring justice to the world at the end of ages. Until then his people warn of this coming cataclysmic judgment and work concurrently against the inhumanities of humanity as a foretaste of that day.

---

39. Moule 1957: 58–59.

RECONCILIATION AND THE COLOSSIANS (1:21–23)

> ²¹ And you who were formerly alienated and enemies in thought by evil deeds, ²² but now he has reconciled you in the body of his flesh through death, to present you as holy and without blemish and irreproachable before him. ²³ If indeed you remain firmly established and steadfast in the faith not swerving from the hope of the gospel which you heard, that has been proclaimed in all of creation under heaven, of which I, Paul, became a servant.

This section brings together both the thanksgiving of 1:3–14 and the Christ Hymn of 1:15–20 by providing further grounds for thanksgiving through the reconciling work of the Messiah as specifically applied to the Colossians. The train of thought in 1:21–23 appears to be: (1) the stark transition the Colossians have experienced in being transferred from enmity and hostility to holiness and hope, (2) the apparent need for the Colossians to remain faithful to the gospel, (3) and the cosmic scope of the gospel. These short verses are significant in so far as they summarize most of the epistle up to this point, including hope and gospel (1:5), worldwide mission (1:6), perseverance (1:11), salvation as transference to a new state (1:12–14), and reconciliation through Jesus's death (1:20). More broadly, the whole section of 1:21—2:7 constitutes a rhetorical *probatio* or logical argument that enumerates the main proposition. Paul here establishes the grounds for their continued adherence to the gospel (as opposed to their acceptance of the philosophy). He does this by setting forth the intrinsic value of what the gospel has already achieved in them, the divine honors accorded to the gospel messengers, and the privileges afforded to those who have been granted access to the divine mystery that centers on the Messiah.

With the mention of **you**, Paul applies the foregoing section to the Colossians directly by involving them in the cosmic saga of reconciliation. Their prior condition is described as **alienated and enemies in thought**, which denotes their active opposition and hostility to God as expressed by their **evil deeds**. These evil deeds probably consist of the set of inappropriate behaviors listed in Col 3:5–9 which typifies the unbelieving Gentile world. This dire condition is then markedly contrasted with the advent of reconciliation. The **now** marks a redemptive-historical transition in the state of the Colossians' relationship to God, which comes through the apocalyptic invasion of the cosmos by God's rectifying work to restore order and justice to the created realm (see Rom 3:21; 6:22; 7:6; 11:30; 1 Cor 15:20). They have been **reconciled**, hostilities and opposition ended, through **the body of his flesh through death**. The words for "body" (*sōma*) and "flesh" (*sarx*) can sometimes be synonymous, but "flesh" normally has negative connotations related to human weakness, frailty, and sinfulness.[1] Yet here they denote, almost crudely, the physicality of Jesus's work involving **death** as the termination of his human life (cf. NET; NIV; NJB).[2] The point is clear: the reconciler is the human Jesus, and the means of reconciliation is his cross. The purpose of Jesus's death is that the Colossians be **presented** before God as **holy and without blemish and irreproachable**. These three descriptions use sacrificial cultic imagery and relate to a particular status rather than to a moral state; it is the absence of guilt or blame that marks those who are reconciled. The **him** of **before him** is indeterminate, it could be Jesus or the Father, but given the preceding context it seems to be a reference to Jesus as the judge on the day of judgment (see John 5:26–30; Acts 17:31; Rom 2:16; 2 Tim 4:1).

This salvation is contingent upon perseverance, as they must remain firmly rooted in the **faith** understood as the received body of Christian teaching. Or, put negatively, **not swerving from the hope of the gospel**, or departing from the hope laid up for them in heaven (1:5). The nature of the Greek "if . . . remain" is a conditional clause and assumes the truthfulness of the proposition set forth; in other words, Paul warns them of failure but seems to presume upon a positive outcome in their

---

1. Cf. Dunn 1996: 107–9; 1998: 55–73.
2. Cf. Lohse 1971: 64; Lincoln 2000: 606.

response.[3] The gospel they are to hold on to is the same one that has been **proclaimed in all of creation under heaven**. Much like what Paul did in 1:6, he puts the Colossians' reception of the gospel in a global and even cosmic context. What is happening to them is a microcosm of what is happening elsewhere in the world. The phrase **all of creation** is certainly hyperbolic, since Paul's missionary endeavors only encompassed selected regions in the eastern Mediterranean from "Jerusalem and as far around as Illyricum" (Rom 15:19). Nonetheless, through the work of **Paul**, God and God's Son were being proclaimed to peoples who knew only the domain of darkness. Indeed, Paul's service has a unique role in the unfolding of the mystery of God, which has recently been made known.

3. Cf. O'Brien 1982: 69; Harris 1991: 60; Dunn 1996: 110; Witherington 2007: 140.

PAUL'S SERVICE:
Messianic Woes, Messianic Mission, and the Messianic Mystery (1:24—2:7)

²⁴ Now I rejoice in my sufferings on your behalf, and in my flesh I am filling up what is lacking in the afflictions of the Messiah, on behalf of his body, that is, the church, ²⁵ which I became a servant according to the commission of God given to me for you, to fulfill the word of God—²⁶the mystery that has been hidden from the ages and from generations, but now has been manifested to his saints. ²⁷ To them God chose to make known how great among the Gentiles are the riches of this glorious mystery, which is Messiah in you, the hope of glory.

²⁸ We proclaim him, admonishing all people and teaching all people in all wisdom, in order that we may present all people mature in Messiah. ²⁹ For this I labor, struggling according to his power which operates in me so mightily. ¹ For I wish you to know how great a struggle I have on behalf of you and for those in Laodicea and for all those who have not seen me in the flesh, ² so that their hearts might be comforted and joined together in love, and have all the riches of full assurance of understanding and the knowledge of the mystery of God, which is the Messiah. ³ In whom are hidden all the treasures of wisdom and knowledge.

⁴ I say this in order that no one might deceive you with persuasive arguments. ⁵ For even if I am absent in the flesh, yet I am with you in spirit, rejoicing to see your orderliness and the firmness of your faithfulness in the Messiah. ⁶ Therefore, as you received Messiah Jesus the Lord, so walk in him, ⁷ being rooted and built up in him and confirmed in the faith just as you were taught, abounding in thanksgiving.

Paul continues the line of thought begun in 1:23 about his apostolic ministry. Paul has given his ministry a cosmic context, but here he attributes to it an apocalyptic function as well. That functions consists of absorbing part of the messianic woes or the travails that fall upon God's people before the final consummation. Such a task is even described as a completion of Jesus's own work. The main themes in this section are the suffering and struggle of the apostolic mission (1:24, 29; 2:1) and the manifestation of God's mystery in the Messiah (1:26–27; 2:2). The final verses (2:4–7) close off this section as an exhortation to avoid deception, to remain faithful in their way of life, and to trust in the Messiah. That itself forms a fitting prelude to Paul's admonition against the Colossian teachers in 2:8–23. Paul is not simply reinforcing the believers' "self-esteem,"[1] but is reinforcing the primary theological fixtures of their faith and reinvigorating their privileges in a shared Christian identity.

Messianic Woes and the Mystery of the Messiah (1:24-27)

Paul continues on from Col 1:23 about the gospel the Colossians have heard and which Paul serves. He adds, **I rejoice in my sufferings on your behalf**. These sufferings are probably the trials, misfortunes, and persecutions referred to elsewhere in Paul's letters (see 1 Cor 4:11–13; 2 Cor 1:3–11; 11:23–30; Phil 1:12–14, 20–26; Acts 9:16) and include synagogue beatings, figuratively facing wild beasts, shipwreck, stoning, imprisonment, and other calamities.[2] These sufferings are said to be **on your behalf** or "for you," but how is this so? Are Paul's sufferings vicarious and redemptive? On the one hand, these sufferings benefit the churches because they are what Paul and his coworkers endure in order to preach the gospel to the world and so his sufferings evidently benefit others. On the other hand, Paul clearly goes further than that when he states, **in my flesh I am filling up what is lacking in the afflictions of the Messiah**, which is also "for" or on **behalf** of the **church**. Does Paul perfect or correct a deficiency in the atoning sufferings of Jesus?[3] Or does Paul see the

1. Dunn 1996: 113–14.

2. Cf. Bird 2008a: 26–28.

3. Calvin (1979a: 166) quotes Augustine's words on the Gospel of John: "Though we brethren die for brethren, yet there is no blood of any martyr that is poured out for the remission of sins. This Christ did for us. Nor has he in this conferred upon us a matter of imitation, but ground of thanksgiving."

sufferings of Christ as symbolic in part for the sufferings of the church via the imagery of corporate personality? Let us consider: (1) the context is dominated by the universal preaching of the gospel and Paul's unique role in that task; (2) the word for "affliction" (*thlipsis*) is never used to describe the atonement, but it can describe the eschatological ordeal of the future age (e.g., Matt 24:9, 21, 29; Mark 13:19, 24; 1 Cor 7:28; Rev 7:14); (3) believers are said to participate in the death of Christ which effectively transfers them from the old age to the new age and marks their identity as being "in Messiah" (e.g., Gal 2:19; Rom 6:5, 11; 8:11; Phil 3:10–11; Col 2:12, 20); and (4) the proclamation of the gospel and the advent of the great apocalyptic tribulation are combined in many places in the New Testament (e.g., Luke 10:17–21; Matt 24:14; Mark 13:10; Rev 14:6). I would follow Richard Bauckham by arguing that what we have here is a Christian reinterpretation of the Jewish idea of a worldwide tribulation, i.e., the "Messianic woes," occasioned by a growing tide of human evil before the final advent of the Messiah. The messianic woes mark the death throes of an old world ending and the birth pangs of a new world beginning.[4]

Christians have reinterpreted this idea in light of the passion of Jesus and the missionary commission of the risen Lord. As the Messiah suffered, so too do his followers suffer as they partake of his afflictions in order to partake of his glory (Rom 8:17; 1 Pet 4:13). His followers also suffer persecution and shame for his name as they bear testimony to his work and person. The two great "not yet" elements of New Testament eschatology, namely, worldwide gospel mission and universal tribulation, are drawn together as the church continues its mission and witness under persecution and opposition.[5] The afflictions of the final day belong to the work of the Messiah, but these are deficient insofar as the work of suffering is incomplete because it lasts until the *parousia* (second coming). Concerning Paul's role specifically, then, Hannah Stettler writes:

> If Paul thought of his ministry as leading to Christ's parousia, Col
> 1:24 seems to express that he sees himself in his apostolic ministry
> as the one who fills up that amount of the suffering set for the

---

4. Bauckham 1975. See also Moule 1957: 76–78; Lohse 1971: 69–71; Martin 1973: 70; O'Brien 1982: 78–79; Wright 1986: 89–90; Dunn 1996: 114–16; H. Stettler 2000; Witherington 2007: 144–45; Bird 2008a: 118; Thompson 2005: 45; contrasted with Barth and Blanke 1994: 292–93; Lincoln 2000: 614; Talbert 2007: 201–2.

5. Cf. Bird 2004.

Church as a whole which is lacking. He does so by being a missionary to the Gentiles. As his mission actually helped to shorten the time before the parousia, the sufferings he encountered as a missionary to the Gentiles served to shorten the time of the messianic woes (cf. Matt 24:21f) . . . This explains how Paul could speak of his sufferings being for the Colossians among whom he had never worked personally. They were "afflictions" because of the identity between Christ and his messenger (cf. 2 Cor 5:20). Paul, as the Servant of the Lord, promoted the coming of the day of the Lord by finishing the Gentile mission, which is a prerequisite of the revelation of the man of lawlessness and the subsequent coming of the Lord linked with the salvation of all of Israel.[6]

Thus, the messianic woes continue to be absorbed by the body of the Messiah, who continues the work of providing a suffering witness and so completes the role that was unfulfilled at the first advent of the Messiah. Paul sees himself as playing a significant part in making up this deficiency through the travails experienced in his apostolic ministry. In fact, Paul reduces the affliction of others such as those in Colossae by absorbing more than his fair share of the corporate sufferings.[7] Yet in these same sufferings emerges the victory of God's kingdom in the service of his cracked and broken vessels of divine grace. As John Chrysostom wrote, Paul's ministry included a mixture of "carnage and trophies."[8] What is more, as James Dunn notes, for such a theology to be realistic Paul would still have to be alive at the time of writing.[9]

Paul goes on to state another element of his apostolate that is for their benefit. He was given the **commission of God** in order to **fulfill the word of God**. Paul's commission has the sense of a task, vocation, stewardship, or office uniquely given to him as part of his divinely ordained role in the revelation of the gospel to the Gentiles (see 1 Cor 4:1; 9:17; Eph 1:10; 3:2, 9). His *raison d'être*, so to speak, was to make the word of God fully and widely known (Gal 1:16; Acts 22:21; 26:17). The word is fulfilled by its effusion into the world (against the NIV's rendering, "word of God in all its fullness"). The Colossians benefit as recipients of the word of God (see

---

6. H. Stettler 2000: 205–6.

7. O'Brien 1982: 80; Wright 1986: 89; Bird 2008a: 118.

8. *Hom. Col.* 1, *NPNF* 13:257.

9. Dunn 1996, 117; cf. H. Stettler 2000: 208.

Col 1:5; 3:16) and as characters in the theodrama of salvation in which they have been destined to participate.

The flow of thought is then interrupted with some remarks about the manifestation of the divine **mystery**.[10] The background to the **mystery** (*mystērion*) is not in the mystery cults or in Gnosticism,[11] but comes from apocalyptic Judaism where "mystery" denoted an intimation of divinely foreordained events that have been deliberately concealed by God (e.g., Dan 2:18–19, 27–30; *1 En.* 51:3; 103:2; at Qumran the Teacher of Righteousness was known as an interpreter of wonderful mysteries, 1QpHab 7:4–5; cf. 1QM 3:9; 1QS 3:21–23). In Paul's unique reckoning this **mystery** is revealed not in the future, but in the recent past, a secret now manifested and broadcast in the preached word of Jesus.[12] This **mystery** is also focused on the Gentiles as recipients of the knowledge that salvation has come to them through the indwelling of the Messiah so that they now share in the **riches of this glorious mystery** (see Eph 1:9; 3:4–6; 6:19). What is so glorious is not the prospect of a disembodied soul one day departing to go to heaven; the glory consists in looking into a hidden plan devised before the ages with the same sense of excitement as children exploring the treasure troves of a lavish palace in a lost city.[13] The concern here pertains to the demystifying of the secret things of God and the disclosure of his plan to bring the Gentiles into the people of God. All this comes through the Messiah taking up residence in and among the nations as the ultimate means to their glory (see Rom 11:25; 16:25–26).[14] The mystery is **Messiah in you**, which is then refined further as **the hope**

10. On *mystērion* in Paul see the judicious study of Bockmuehl 1990.

11. Cf. McL. Wilson (2005: 175): "As for *mystērion* itself, too much should not be read into the use of this word, in the sense of influence from the mystery religions on a nascent Christianity."

12. Lohse 1971: 74. See also 1QS 11.5–8 where the mystery refers to an event that has already taken place, such as the Qumran community's participation in the angelic assembly (Lincoln 2000: 615). A similar link of "mystery" and angel worship could be propagated by the teachers at Colossae.

13. Wright 1986: 92.

14. According to Bruce (1957: 218 n. 168) there are two distinct, but related aspects to the mystery in Ephesians and Colossians. In Colossians it is the fact that the indwelling of Messiah is for Gentiles as well as Jews. Whereas in Ephesians, the mystery is that in the Messiah, Gentile believers are fellow heirs with Jewish believers. Dunn (1996: 121) comments: "For as Eph. 3:4–6 shows, the two thoughts (the mystery of Jew and Gentile together as recipients of God's saving grace and the mystery of Christ) are two aspects of the same larger divine plan as Paul had come to see it." See also Moule 1957: 82–83.

of glory. The **you** most probably describes Gentiles who have entered into the citizenship of Israel.[15] Clearly the fulcrum of the mystery is the person and work of Jesus, so that the glory that was lost at the fall of the old creation is regained through the new Adam and bestowed upon participants in the new creation. Humanity is reconfigured and renewed into its former glorious Edenic state in the Messiah. Polemically put, the mystery of God is made known through the gospel of the Messiah and not in the intellectual structures of Judaism, Hellenistic philosophy, Jewish magic, or in the esoteric revelations reported by mystics (Col 2:18). In contrast to the teachers, the mystery of heaven is not found in visionary ascents to the heavenly throne, but it consists in the life of heaven coming down and falling upon Jews and Gentiles through the indwelling of the Messiah.

MISSIONARY STRUGGLES AND THE MYSTERY OF THE MESSIAH (1:28—2:3)

Part of Paul's strategy to commend their continued obedience to the gospel is to show the Colossians how they belong to a wider network of churches spread across the world, and that the most glorious mysteries of the universe have been given to them in Jesus the Messiah. The universality of the Pauline mission is emphasized by **all people** (*panta anthrōpon*), which is repeated three times. Emphasis falls upon the medium and intent of Paul's teaching ministry and that of his coworkers (hence the switch to the plural **we**).[16] This includes **proclaiming him**, evangelistic activity focused on Jesus; **admonishing**, understood as warning or correction; and **teaching**, as imparted learning in the way of Jesus. These efforts result in people being **mature in Messiah**. Persons who are gospelized in this way attain the full maturity of spiritual renewal that comes from living in the purposes of God (see Col 4:12; Eph 4:13). This maturing is tantamount to being conformed to the image of God's Son (Rom 8:29; 2 Cor 3:18) and the new self being renewed according to the image of its creator (Col 3:10).[17] Such maturation or perfection comes through the preced-

15. Cf. Lohse 1971: 76; Wolter 1993: 105; Bockmuehl 1990: 182.

16. This universality clearly stands over and against the philosophy of the Colossian teachers. See Lightfoot 1879: 168; Abbott 1897: 235; Bruce 1957: 219; Sappington 1991: 186.

17. Alternatively, **present mature** may refer to the *parousia* and how Paul hopes that the Colossians will be "blameless" on the day of Christ Jesus. See O'Brien 1982: 89–90.

ing activity of proclamation, admonition, and instruction. To paraphrase Markus Barth, to be mature means to cling to the promise of the gospel with unshakable trust in the Messiah and to cleave to the promise in him because it is identical to him. There is no maturing or perfecting other than that attained through trust in and faithfulness to the Messiah.[18] Paul then returns again to the umbilical connection between his mission and the struggles that he faces in the execution of the apostolic vocation. Paul's struggle, including absorbing the messianic woes, is a **labor** that may seem insurmountable, but is dramatically effective through divine empowerment. The Greek phrasing in 1:29 is awkward and tautologous, but it emphatically underscores the efficacy of the divine power that operates in Paul to achieve its designed purpose. The **power** (*energeia*) that energizes Paul is the same that raised Jesus from the dead (2:12). Paul prayed earlier that the Colossians would be "strengthened with all power according to his glorious might," (1:11) which is an ideal that he embodies for their aspiration and imitation.

For the first time, Paul mentions the believers in **Laodicea** and others who have not seen him **in the flesh**, which is probably most or all of the believers in the Lycus Valley. The purpose of this report is not Paul's self-adulation, rather, the news of triumph in the face of adversity is given so that **their hearts might be comforted** specifically by means of **being joined together in love**. That is to say, hearing that they are united in the worldwide movement of the Messiah, bound by a common baptism, sharing a common salvation, united in bonds of affection, and sharing in the new creation, is a means to comfort their hearts in periods of perplexity. Encouragement is required in the context of internal wranglings caused by exposure to Jewish teachers who raise doubts within their ranks about their assured standing before God. The Colossians possess **full assurance** because in their apprehension of the **mystery of God** they apprehend the **Messiah** (see the "mystery of Messiah" in Col 4:3). Precisely in the Messiah they already have the **wisdom** and **knowledge** that they seek or are told to seek. The same language of knowledge and wisdom is found in Jewish traditions related to the Torah (4 Macc 1:16–17; Sir 24:1–23; Bar 3:15—4:1; 2 *Bar.* 44:14; 54:13). This accords with the Jewish nature of the philosophy that attaches wisdom and knowledge to the Torah, whereas

18. Barth and Blanke 1994: 267.

Paul unites these two entities in Jesus.[19] Paradoxically, this knowledge is **hidden** and yet also unraveled in the **Messiah**, as he embodies the wisdom and secret things of God.

EXHORTATION TO FAITHFULNESS IN THE MESSIAH (2:4–7)

Although Paul has already intimated his exhortation and warning at earlier points, he begins his first formal exhortatory section here. This section in Col 2:4–7 rounds off Col 1:1—2:3 and more closely relates to what has gone before than to what follows. It functions like a *conplexio* that briefly recaps the argument up to this point. The apostle and his coauthor denigrate the philosophy further by their remarks and urge faithfulness and continuance in the pattern of teaching that the Colossians first received. The undergirding principle is to hold on to that which accords with the image and power of the Messiah as explicated in the poem of 1:15–20.

Paul relates **this**, that is, what has just been written or read out pertaining to the sufficiency and supremacy of the Messiah for the Colossians, **in order that no one might deceive you with persuasive arguments**. The obvious impression is that Paul is fireproofing the Colossians against perceived error. The philosophy has not gained a foothold yet, but Paul and his coworkers are intent on preventing any further encroachment.[20] These **persuasive arguments** (*pithanologia*, see "fine-sounding" [NIV], "plausible" [NRSV; ESV], "specious" [NJB]) refer to views and practices that sound attractive and alluring, but in fact adherence to them removes the Colossians from their root and foundation in the Messiah. While Paul is **absent** in person, he is there in **spirit**. He is present with them because both he and they live in Messiah and share in the Spirit of God. Paul wants to see (or hear about) the Colossians' endurance, steadfastness, and **faithfulness in the Messiah** (see Col 1:4, 11, 23). The words for **orderliness** (*taxis*) and **firmness** (*stereōma*) can be used generally in exhortations, but also in military terminology for fortifications (e.g., Xenophon *Anab.* 1.2.18). Taking this latter sense, the imagery is of preparedness for conflict and of loyalty to one's commander. Paul's inferential **Therefore** begins the assigned imperative that follows. Their fidelity to what they **received** about the **Messiah Jesus the Lord** is a model for how they are now

19. O'Brien 1982: 96; Bockmuehl 1990: 188–90; Beale 2007: 855.
20. Cf. Martin 1973: 77; O'Brien 1982: 99.

to live. Paul returns to the halakic metaphor of 1:10 ("walk worthily of the Lord") by urging them to **walk in him**, which is equivalent to remaining loyal to and grounded in the faith that they were first **taught**. Such fidelity is incomplete of course unless it is accompanied with **thanksgiving**. In this way, Paul links together their beliefs and social identity as followers of Jesus with their devotional life as well.

Paul clearly wants to shore up the actual content of what the Colossians hold to by arguing for the sufficiency of the knowledge and wisdom contained in **the faith** they received. Much like Gal 3:1–5, he wants them to add nothing to the faith and hope that they have begun in. But another significant component of Paul's strategy is to remind the Colossians that their identity is bound up with a network of other believers spread across adjacent regions. The sufferings and strife of the other churches is for them, and they are partners in that struggle. Paul's narration of his apostolic ministry is not a self-congratulatory digression but is intrinsic to his argument, as he must persuade an audience that he does not know directly the relevance of his office and his message for their particular context.[21] Paul defends the gospel in Colossae by reiterating their *solidarity* with other believers and by emphasizing the *sufficiency* of their faith. They are also beneficiaries of the mystery of God made known to them in knowledge of the Messiah. The dispute in Colossae, or at least Paul and his coworker's perception of it, ultimately revolves around what they have received about the Messiah and who they are in the Messiah.

21. Cf. MacDonald 2008: 89.

ENGAGING THE EMPTY DECEIT OF A MYSTIC JUDAISM IN A HELLENISTIC PHILOSOPHICAL GARB (2:8–23)

[8] See to it that no one takes you captive by philosophy and empty deceit, according to human tradition, according to the elemental forces of the cosmos and not according to Messiah. [9] For in him the fulness of deity dwells bodily, [10] and you have been filled in him, who is the head of every ruler and authority. [11] In him you were also circumcised with a circumcision done without human hands, in putting off the body of flesh in the circumcision of the Messiah. [12] Having been buried with him in baptism, in which you were also raised with him through faith in the operation of God, who raised him from the dead. [13] And you, who were dead in the trespasses and the uncircumcision of your flesh, God made you alive with him, having forgiven us all of our trespasses, [14] having erased the manuscript, with its decrees, which stood against us; he took it from our midst, having nailed it to the cross. [15] He disarmed the rulers and authorities and put them to public shame, triumphing over them in the cross.

[16] Therefore, let no one judge you in matters of food and drink or with regard to a feast or a New Moon or a Sabbath, [17] which are merely a shadow of what is to come, but the substance belongs to the Messiah. [18] Let no one disqualify you, insisting on ascetic practices and worship of angels, which he has purportedly seen on entering (heaven), vainly being puffed up by his fleshly mind, [19] and not grasping the head, from whom the whole body is supplied and joined together through its joints and ligaments, it grows with a growth that is of God. [20] If you died with Messiah to the elemental forces

of the cosmos, why, as if you were living in the world, do you continue to submit to its regulations? [21] "Do not handle do not taste, do not touch" [22] (which marks all things which perish as they are used up), according to the commandments and teachings of men? [23] These indeed have an appearance of wisdom in promoting pseudo-piety and ascetic practices and harsh treatment of the body, but they are not of any value in restraining the gratification of the flesh.

In this section we come to the hub of Paul's attack on the philosophy. To an audience listening to the letter read out aloud, 2:8–23 would sound like the *refutatio* of a deliberative discourse by striking up arguments against an opposing viewpoint. Paul engages the philosophy of the teachers in Colossae in this unit, and his critique, especially its language and background, bears a semblance to his earlier critique of worldly philosophy in 1 Corinthians and his attack on Judeo-Christian nomism in Galatians. Paul is not simply rehearsing older debates, nor are the issues faced in Colossae identical to those in Corinth or Galatia. More likely, Paul and his coworkers draw on a repertoire of debates and polemics from earlier episodes to combat a perceived encroachment upon a Gentile Christian community in Colossae. In 2:8, Paul clearly sets up a contrast of philosophy, human tradition, and elemental forces on the one hand and the Messiah on the other hand. The Messiah is emphasized as a figure who embodies deity, transforms persons through an inner circumcision symbolized by baptism, cancels the condemnatory regulations of the Torah, and defeats hostile spiritual powers through his cross. In contrast, the philosophy is associated with submission to malevolent powers, the manuscript with its decrees, needlessly harsh ascetic practices, the worship of/with angels, adhering to various prohibitions pertaining to cultic matters, accepting claims of wisdom, listening to reports of visions, and restraining fleshly desires through mistreatment of the body. As stated in the introduction, the philosophy clearly has a Jewish flavor, with references to circumcision, New Moon festivals, and Sabbath keeping. All features of the philosophy can be paralleled in Jewish beliefs and practices of the Second Temple period. For Paul, the goal of the Torah has reached its completion in Jesus, so that to turn to the Torah for the basis of their identity, way of life, or salvation is to return to an obsolete and even oppressive situation (see Rom 10:4; Gal 3:1–5).

The thrust of Paul's argument is that the true meaning of the Colossian believers' identification with the Messiah is freedom from the exact kinds of practices being foisted upon them. What is more, the philosophy does not deliver on what it promises; its rituals, regulations, and esoteric experiences are ineffective. The philosophy does not enhance their standing and prestige before God, but rather hinders it. Its claims have a human rather than heavenly origin. The various proscriptions of the teachers derive from a false and manufactured piety. The vision reports are self-inflationary, not revelatory or edifying. Even worse, the philosophy results in a secondary submission to malevolent forces after the Messiah has already released believers from bondage. This critique comes through an interweaving of Christology, eschatology, and cosmology, where Paul sets up the Messiah as a type of master of the universe who has emancipated an annexed territory and freed the inhabitants from the decrees of their former overlords.

The section is structured around reference to the claims of the teachers in Colossae and the counterclaims of Paul in regards to the futility of the philosophy and the fullness of the Messiah (2:8–15). He then admixes some exhortatory comments with three major prohibitions that result in behavior that moves them away from the philosophy and back towards an ethical paradigm more in line with the gospel (2:16–23). In many ways, it is an extension of the *propositio* set forth in 1:15–20 concerning the sufficiency of supremacy of the Messiah.

THE COLOSSIAN PHILOSOPHY AS CAPTIVITY AND THE WORK OF MESSIAH AS CONQUEST (2:8–15)

Paul commences his exhortation with regards to the **philosophy**[1] more directly, and both segments of his thought (2:8, 16) begin with injunctions that **no one** (*mē tis*)[2] pressure them into certain behaviors or attitudes

---

1. Many things could pass as a **philosophy** in the ancient world, including certain schools of philosophy (Platonism, Stoicism, Pythagoreanism, Cynicism, etc.), religions such as Judaism, the study of magic, and mystery religions. It is probable that **philosophy** represents the teachers' own designation of their body of teachings and way of life.

2. Paul can often refer to his opponents obliquely as "some," "certain men," or "those" (Rom 3:8; 1 Cor 4:18; 15:12, 34; 2 Cor 3:1; 10:2; Gal 1:7; 2:12; Phil 1:15). But one should

inconsistent with faith in the Messiah. The first injunction is that they not be taken **captive by philosophy and empty deceit**, where the philosophy is depicted as intellectually void in content and devious in nature (see 1 Cor 3:18; Eph 5:6). Interestingly, the word for **captive** (*sulagōgeō*) sounds remarkably similar to the word for "synagogue" (*synagōgē*) with perhaps a deliberate play on words.[3] This would underscore, albeit obliquely, the Jewish nature of the philosophy being commended to the Colossian Christians. In other words, Paul implies, do not let yourself be captured, kidnapped, and dragged off by the local synagogue for indoctrination.

The failings of the philosophy are then explained further. First, it is according to **human tradition**, which was a common Christian jibe at certain Jewish expansive interpretations of the Torah, i.e., specific suggestions as to what it means to obey the law of Moses (see Mark 7:8; Gal 1:14). What is being proscribed is perhaps a feature of Jewish halakah, or traditions of interpretation and application pertaining to the Old Testament regulations passed on by Jewish religious leaders (which makes sense of the prescriptions about holy days and prohibited foods in 2:16, 21).[4] These prescribed practices demand stringent adherence to a rigid set of teachings that aims to ensure complete obedience to God. Yet Paul objects to Gentile Christians having their freedom curtailed by Torah and its accompanying interpretation by religious groups in Colossae. In the words of Andrew Lincoln: "For Colossians the gospel is grace, and no response to it can depart from the foundation by adding human achievements as a requirement. Instead, authentic Christian living is motivated by a response to and empowered by an appropriation of the undeserved favor of God in Christ."[5] Second, the philosophy is **according to the elemental forces of the cosmos**, or perhaps, "accords with certain principalities and powers." The identity of the **elemental forces** (*stoicheia*) is somewhat debatable (see Gal 4:3, 9). They can refer to the basic principles of some-

---

not infer here, as Dunn (1996: 146) does, that the use of the future tense (*estai*, "it will be") suggests a "possibility" as opposed to a "current state of affairs." See in contrast Lightfoot 1879: 178; Abbott 1897: 246; Lincoln 2000: 662; McL. Wilson 2005: 194.

3. Wright 1986: 100.

4. We should note, however, that Greek philosophy could also talk about handing on traditions (see Lohse 1971: 95 n. 24). Arnold (1996: 188, 204–10) points out that magical incantations could also be described as "traditions" too. Arnold's attempt to press "wisdom," "philosophy," and "tradition" into the aid of a magical background seems too forced.

5. Lincoln 2000: 576–77.

thing (Heb 5.12) or to the material substances of the universe—earth, water, air, and fire (2 Pet 3:10, 12; Wis 7:17; 19:18).[6] A further option is to see them as cosmic powers. In line with this, fragmentary horoscopes have been found in the Qumran writings that depict celestial bodies as having a determining force (4Q186; 4Q534), and ancient persons were interested in the power of astral planes and heavenly beings in controlling their destiny.[7] Jewish apocalyptic literature had already begun closely associating the angels with the elements of the heavenly bodies (4 Ezra 6:3; *Jub.* 2:2; *1 En.* 60:11–12; 74:1; *2 En.* 4:1; *T. Ab.* 13:11).[8] Most likely, the **elemental forces** denote hostile angelic entities equivalent to the "rulers" and "authorities" mentioned elsewhere in Colossians (1:16; 2:15). The description **elemental forces of the cosmos** might even be Paul's own designation for angelic mediators that require adoration, appeasement, and provide access to divine worship.[9] In Galatians, the angels are explicitly linked to the giving of the law at Sinai (Gal 3:19; cf. Acts 7:53; Heb 2:2) showing that imposition of the law and the authority of the angels are directly associated. Also in Galatians, Paul likens Gentiles turning to the Torah to secure some form of protection, perfection, or prize as being equivalent to a return to slavery under pagan deities. The words of Theodoret of Cyr, though in the distant fifth century, are still relevant: "Those who defend the law lead persons to worship angels, since they say that the law was given through them. This vice persisted for a long time in Phrygia and Pisidia, such that a synod gathered at Laodicea in Phrygia laid down that angels should be not invoked."[10] It is possible that the philosophy has drawn on Jewish traditions about angels delivering the law and angelic authority over the cosmic elements in order to commend their religious practices to the Christians in Colossae in some esoteric

---

6. Cf. G. Delling, *TDNT* 8:666–83; O'Brien 1982: 129–32; Sappington 1991: 164–68; Barth and Blanke 1994: 373–78.

7. Kee 2005: 470–72.

8. The document *Testament of Solomon* describes Solomon's encounter with several spirits who describe themselves thus: "We are the elements, the cosmic rulers of darkness" (8:2), and "We are the thirty-six elements, the cosmic rulers of darkness of this age" (18:2). There is also the text from Vettius Valens 7.5: "I adjure you by Helios and Selene, and by the courses of the five stars . . . and by the four *stoicheia*" (cited from Arnold 1996: 165).

9. Cf. Barclay 1997: 51.

10. Gorday 2000: 39.

mix of angel veneration and asceticism.[11] In 2:20, then, Paul asserts that dying with the Messiah releases believers from the grip of these forces and their prescribed practices. Third, the philosophy is not **according to Messiah**, which is to say that it does not correspond with the teaching about the Messiah received by the Colossians that is defined elsewhere as the "word of Messiah" (3:16) or "the faith" (1:23; 2:7).

Paul proceeds to justify the superiority of the Messiah to the philosophy in a number of ways. To begin with, he states that **in him the fulness of deity dwells bodily**, which should be taken as a reference to the incarnation.[12] The adverb **bodily** (*sōmatikōs*) indicates the mechanism through which God dwells in the Messiah. Paul emphasizes the body of the Messiah by referring to his bodily death (1:22), bodily resurrection (2:11–12), and bodily exaltation (3:1).[13] No angelic figure measures up to him as he is identified in a unique and absolute way with the God of the universe. Access to the divine realm is not attained through a philosophically savvy spin on Judaism with angelic furnishings, but through the God-in-Christ event, whereby the body of the Messiah becomes the very locus of God's holy presence and saving activity. Thus, Jesus is not merely another cosmic aeon or angelic intermediary, but the self-revelation of God in human form. If we read 2:9 in light of 1:15–20, it means that the divine nature did not dwell in Jesus only after his resurrection, but resided in the one in whom the cosmic powers were created and in whom the whole universe finds coherence.[14] Accordingly, solidarity with the Messiah means participation in the divine life and the divine power of creation and new creation that is embodied in him.

Paul turns and says that the Colossians **have been filled in him**, specifying not what they are filled with, but in whom they are filled. The chief thought is of fulfillment or completion of communion with God by union with the Messiah. The same one who is the embodiment of the divine presence is also sovereign over every **ruler and authority**. These entities occur here in the singular, whereas they are used in the plural elsewhere (i.e., rulers and authorities in 1:16; 2:15), but little can be made of that distinction. The main point, as in the Christ Hymn, is that Jesus is

11. Dunn 1996: 151.
12. Contra e.g., Scott 1930: 43.
13. Wall 1993: 111.
14. Kooten 2003: 25.

sovereign and supreme over the very "powers" that the Colossians think that they could appease through partial Torah observance.

The meaning and significance of being **in him** is further unpacked through a number of metaphors that emphasize their incorporation into the Messiah.[15] Starting with a cultic metaphor, it means that one has been **circumcised with a circumcision done without human hands**. The mention of **circumcision** would bring to mind a number of things to any reader familiar with Israel's sacred traditions. Circumcision of male babies on the eighth day was the seal of God's covenant with Abraham, the sign of membership in the Mosaic covenant, and a catchword for the Jewish people. The Old Testament scriptures also know of a "spiritual" circumcision (Deut 10:16; 30:6; Jer 4:4; Ezek 44:7) and such a thought lies in the background here. It is applied by Paul to those who are physically uncircumcised themselves, but have been ingrafted into the commonwealth of Israel through the Messiah of Israel (see Rom 2:28–29; 2 Cor 3:3; Phil 3:3; *Gos. Thom.* 53; *Odes Sol.* 11:2). A **circumcision done without human hands** most likely refers to the regenerating work of the Holy Spirit in the believer.[16] Things made with **human hands**, in Jewish tradition, were the manufacturing of idols and pagan temples (Lev 26:1; Isa 45:16).[17] While it is possible to find here a critique of circumcision being forced upon Gentiles, it is by no means certain that the teachers were urging circumcision.[18] Given that circumcision is used rhetorically rather than singled out specifically in relation to the philosophy, the teachers were most likely after adherents rather than full converts. More to the point, this messianic work of circumcision signifies an act of renewal and appears to be divided into two parts. On the one side, there is **putting off the body of flesh**, which is tantamount to turning from paganism and idolatry towards the living God (see 1 Thess 1:9). On the other side, there is also the **circumcision of the Messiah**, which most likely pertains to the circumcision done by the Messiah and which characterizes those who belong to the Messiah, that is to say, a messianic circumcision of the heart that brings new life.[19]

15. Cf. O'Brien 1982: 114; Dunn 1996: 152–70.

16. In my view this **circumcision** refers to regeneration and not to water baptism. See for discussion Barth and Blanke 1994: 363–69; Harris 1991: 103; and esp. Hunt 1990.

17. On the possibility of a Stoic background to "without human hands" see Schweizer 1982: 141 n. 22.

18. Note the similar sentiments of MacDonald 2008: 99.

19. A number of commentators (Martin 1973: 82–83; O'Brien 1982: 117; Dunn

The implications are largely eschatological and ethical. This circumcision marks a moment of eschatologial fulfilment, as the Messiah has done for the uncircumcised flesh what the circumcision of the flesh accomplished for Israel. That marks the liberation of the circumcised and uncircumcised from the dark vestiges of the flesh. This comes not from Torah, but from Messiah.[20]

Paul then mentions his second metaphor, **baptism**, which emblematizes how believers were **buried with him** and also **raised with him**. The imagery of baptism represents believers mimetically sharing in the event of Jesus's passion by descending into the waters as per his death and burial and then surfacing from the waters marking his resurrection into new life. The whole ritual served to highlight their experience of participation in the Messiah's passion and vivification by the Father (see Rom 6:4–6; Eph 2:5–6). The instrument of this is **faith in the operation of God**. The life-giving power of God in raising his Son from the dead is also operative in the believer who has faith in the Messiah. Notable faith is directed towards what God has done in the event of the death and resurrection of his Son with attention given to its salvific benefits. This baptismal symbolism is equally applicable because the believers themselves, formerly pagans, were **dead in the trespasses and the uncircumcision of your flesh** and thus alienated and hostile to their Creator. Their pre-faith state of being uncircumcised in the flesh as idol worshipping Gentiles wallowing in death stands in marked contrast to their current state of being circum-

---

1996: 158; Lincoln 2000: 623–24; Thompson 2005: 56–57; Barth and Blanke 1994: 364–65; Hunt 1990: 241–42; Smith 2006: 144) see **circumcision of the Messiah** as referring to Jesus's death. This makes sense given that Paul refers to union with Messiah in circumcision, burial, and resurrection in vv. 11–12, whereas in Romans 6 Paul refers to sharing in Jesus's death, burial, and resurrection. Yet I would maintain that (1) **circumcision of the Messiah** is coordinate to **putting off the body of flesh** and is the opposite of **the uncircumcision of your flesh** in v. 13. The content of v. 11 then does not stand for the indicative (death of Jesus) and imperative (putting off evil deeds) elements, but underscores the transformative power of being in-Messiah. Paul is giving a messianic rewording to "circumcision of the heart." (2) The actual indicative aspect of Paul's exhortation is provided in vv. 12–15, while v. 11 states the reality that is created by Jesus's triumphant death. (3) Any attempt to find an identical linear sequence akin to Romans 6 fails because baptism in v. 12 encompasses death and resurrection with Jesus and in v. 13 it is their spiritual death and spiritual quickening that is in view. (4) There seems to be a two-stage scheme of participation based on baptism/burial (= death) and resurrection in vv. 12–13, and there is no wooden imitation of the pattern in Romans 6. See further Calvin1979a: 184; Schweizer 1982: 143; Harris 1991: 103; Pokorný 1991: 124–25.

20. Schweizer 1982: 142.

cised with a circumcision without human hands. Paul will have much more to say about that contrast in Col 3:1–12, but now the life of God comes via being **made alive with him**. To have life is to be in the Messiah. In fact, in 3:4 Paul says the Messiah is "your life," and this life in the here and now is accessible through being **forgiven** (see 1:14). Forgiveness itself stands with redemption, new exodus, reconciliation, and participation as one of the many metaphors for salvation in Colossians.

At this crucial moment in his argument, Paul refers back to the cross as the grounds for forgiveness and the instrument of divine victory over evil. Paul continues his explication of the superiority of the Messiah over the philosophy with reference to the cross, but now casts it in cosmic and triumphalistic terms. Jesus has **erased the manuscript**, which is characterized as making claims stated in certain **decrees**[21] that are **against us**. The metaphor is undoubtedly legal as the word *cheirographon* literally means the written receipt of a debt owed (cf. "certificate of debt" NASB; "bond" RSV).[22] But here the word takes on a decidedly ethical meaning related to behavioral obligations put in written form that persons are somehow evaluated against. So what exactly is this **manuscript**? There are a number of options. (1) A heavenly book recording the various deeds of persons upon which they are held to account on the day of reckoning. Such books are attested in the Jewish Scriptures and developed in apocalyptic literature (Exod 32:32–33; Ps 69:28; Dan 12:1; Rev 3:5; cf. *Jub.* 4:23; 39:6; *1 En.* 81:2–4; 89:61–64, 70–71; 96:7; 97:5–7; 104:7; 108:7; *2 En.* 44:5–7; 50:1; 52:15; 53:2–3; *Apoc. Ab.* 7:1–8; *Apoc. Zeph.* 3:6–9; 7:1–11; *Apoc. Paul* 17). (2) What is more likely, however, is that it refers to the Torah, or at least Torah's claim to render condemnation over persons for their transgressions. The teachers combine Torah and their specific teachings in 2:21–22, which are then linked to "judging" others in 2:16.[23] But could

21. The **decrees** (*dogma*, cf. 2:20 *dogmatizō*) could refer to the rules within a philosophical system like Pythagoreanism, but the same word can stand for "commandments" pertaining to the Torah (e.g., 3 Macc 1.3; Josephus *Ag. Ap.* 1.42; Philo *Leg.* 1.55; *Gig.* 52). The word occurs in Eph 2:15 where it is explicitly linked to the Mosaic law, i.e., "the law with its commandments and decrees."

22. Cf. *LightAE* 334–36; E. Lohse, *TDNT* 9:435; N. Walter, *EDNT* 3:464.

23. Abbott 1897: 255; Bruce 1957: 237 n. 58; 1984d: 296; Wright 1986: 112; Harris 1991: 107–8. Several patristic authors (e.g., John Chrysostom, Theodore of Mopsuestia, Severian of Gabala) also see a reference to the Old Testament law here (Gorday 2000: 33). Lightfoot (1879: 187) takes the decrees as "though referring primarily to the Mosaic ordinances, will include all forms of positive decrees in which moral or social principles are

a first-century Jew speak of the divinely given law in such terms? Paul and the law is one of the most complex and difficult subjects of Pauline theology and the history of early Christianity. For Paul, the Torah is part of the tripartite structure of law-sin-death (1 Cor 15:56), which, in the saga of redemptive history, makes the law a hostile power exerting a deadly force upon human beings. This is why Paul can associate the Torah with wrath (Rom 4:15), sin (Rom 5:20), slavery (Rom 7:6, 25; Gal 4:1–7; 5:1), death (2 Cor 3:6–7), curses (Gal 3:10), imprisonment (Rom 7:6; Gal 3:22–23), a temporary but harsh guardianship (Gal 3:24), and even depict it as hostile spiritual power (Gal 4:8–10). That is not to say that Torah is intrinsically evil; to the contrary, Paul regards it as good, just, and holy (Rom 7:12). The Torah became an instrument of death only through sin and it was designed to be in effect only until the coming of the Messiah. In the hands of certain "powers" the law becomes a tool of oppression and captivity. It is from the "sting," "curse," and "condemnation" of this manuscript that believers are delivered.

Paul's statements about freedom and liberation from the law elsewhere stand in analogy to his claim that Jesus **took it from our midst**, rather like taking a gun or knife out of the hand of an assailant. Through the metaphor of a triumph, that is, a formal procession celebrating a military victory, Paul reverses the image of the cross as an emblem of shame and defeat and transforms it into one of honor and victory (see 2 Cor 2:14). The angelic powers that seek to use the Torah to subjugate the believers find the weapon snatched from their grasp and **nailed** to **the cross**. The penalty and curse of the Torah is undone as its punitive effects are absorbed in the flesh of the Son of God (see Rom 8:3; Gal 3:13). Without the power of sin and law, the powers are now **disarmed**[24] as their single arrow to threaten and kill has been broken in the body of the Messiah. Thus, he renders them impotent and victimless as their power is spent and broken.

---

embodied or religious duties defined."

24. I demur from the view of some (e.g., Lightfoot 1879: 190; Moule 1957: 101; McL. Wilson 2005: 211–12) that Christ stripped or divested himself of something like his flesh or the powers as if they were a form of clothing (cf. the Gnostic *Gospel of Truth*: "Having stripped himself of the perishable rags, he put on imperishability . . . he passed through those who were stripped naked by oblivion"). I prefer to take the participle *apekdusamenos* as "having disarmed" and regard the middle voice as deponent (see Lohse 1971: 112; Gnilka 1980: 142; Bruce 1984d: 297–98; Arnold 1996: 278; BDF § 316.1). Stanley Porter (1994: 69) states that "Jesus Christ's beneficial or participatory stripping of the defeated demonic enemies of their power makes better sense of the imagery."

In the **cross**,[25] a vulgar means of execution that expressed the zenith of death, disempowerment, and degradation, Jesus has triumphed over cosmic evil and struck a fatal blow to despots of malevolence. Their defeat comes not from an armada of angels led by an archangel or by a Messiah who rides a fiery chariot at the head of a coalition of the willing, but in the apex of human suffering and shame. In Jewish thinking the final defeat of evil and the triumph of Yahweh over the forces of evil was scheduled for a future day; something that Paul affirms elsewhere (e.g. Rom 16:20; 1 Cor 15:24–27). However, here the epic battle and the victory of God are not projected to the future, but are located in the past event of the crucifixion. The execution of Jesus has become a triumphal procession;[26] it is where the powers have been put to **public shame** and made a spectacle for all to see. This is called the *Christus Victor* motif, which regards Jesus's death as the victory of God over evil in all of its hideous forms, whether demonic, political, human, or cosmic.[27] Tom Wright is eminently quotable:

> The "rulers and authorities" of Rome and of Israel—as Caird points out, the best government and the highest religion of the world that time had ever known—conspired to place Jesus on the cross. These powers, angry at his challenge to their sovereignty, stripped *him* naked, held *him* up to public contempt, and celebrated a triumph over *him*. In one of his most dramatic statements of the paradox of the cross, and one moreover which shows in what physical detail Paul could envisage the horrible death Jesus had died, he declares that, on the contrary, on the cross God was stripping *them* naked, was holding *them* to public contempt, and leading *them* in his own triumphal procession—in Christ, the crucified Messiah. When the "powers" had done their worst, crucifying the lord of glory *incognito* on the charge of blasphemy and rebellion, they have overreached themselves. He, neither blasphemer nor rebel, was in fact their rightful sovereign. They thereby exposed themselves for what they were—usurpers of the authority which was properly his. The cross therefore becomes the source of hope for all who had been held captive under their rule, enslaved in fear and mutual

---

25. It is possible that the personal pronoun *autō* in v. 15 could mean "in him" (RSV, ESV, NASB) or "in it" (KJV, NRSV) with "it" meaning "by the cross" (NIV, NIB, NET). It seems likely to me that the dative pronoun in v. 15 relates back to the dative "by the cross" (*tō staur tō*) in v. 14.

26. On the imagery of a triumphal procession see Williams 1999: 257–60.

27. Cf. Boyd 2006; McKnight 2007: 110.

suspicion. Christ breaks the last hold that the "powers" had over his people, by dying on their behalf. He now welcomes them into a new family in which the ways of the old world—its behaviour, its distinctions of race and class and sex, its blind obedience to the "forces" of politics and economics, prejudice and superstition—have become quite simply out of date, a ragged and defeated rabble.[28]

The sequence of metaphors is stunning and powerful. In the circumcision of the Messiah the old uncircumcised flesh is stripped away and a new person is brought to life. The power of the Messiah's passion flows over into believers as they share in his death and resurrection through baptism. The decrees and condemnation of the Torah are singularly swept aside through his atoning death. Finally, the cosmic powers that use Torah to oppress are disarmed and paraded as captive fugitives and reduced to little more than tokens of the Messiah's triumphant reign. Thus, there is more at stake and more blessings available from being "in him" than what adherence to the philosophy offers.

THE POWER OF UNION WITH THE MESSIAH AND THE IMPOTENCE OF THE TORAH (2:16–23)

If the works of the Messiah are eminently superior to the works of the philosophy, then that carries with it a number of corollaries that Paul spells out, hence **therefore**. Paul unpacks what this means now to the claims of the teachers and the way of life that they are urging the Colossians to follow. To begin with, they must let **no one judge** them with the sense of condemn or pass judgment over. Such language belongs to a context of intra-Jewish debates where there could be severe evaluations about whether certain disputed practices were in accordance with the law or not, i.e., disputes about halakah or interpretive matters related to daily living (see Luke 6:37/Matt 7:1; John 8:15; Rom 2:1; 14:3–4, 10, 13; Jas 4:12). This fits with the following descriptions that relate the judgment to **matters of food and drink or with regard to a feast or a New Moon or a Sabbath**. The triadic formula (feasts, New Moon, and Sabbath) occurs in the Septuagint and represents the commandments of the Torah.[29] The

28. Wright 1986: 116–17; see also Walsh and Keesmaat 2004: 111.

29. Hos 2:13; Ezek 45:17; 1 Chron 23:31; 2 Chron 2:3; 31:3; and *Jub.* 1:14. This renders highly improbable Arnold's (1996: 214–18) attempt to link the expression with magic.

matters pertaining to **food** designate the Jewish laws detailing clean and unclean foods (Lev 11:1–23; Deut 14:3–21). Adherence to the food laws was a matter of purity and election since they kept the Israelites separate from the other nations and preserved their capacity to worship God in a state of ritual purity. Adherence to the food laws was a key indicator of loyalty to the covenant especially during the Hellenistic period when Hellenism was being violently thrust upon Judeans in the second century BCE (1 Macc 1:62–63; Tob 1:10–12; Jdt 12:2, 19; *Jos. Asen.* 7:1; 8:5). The Jewish dietary practices publicized Jewish distinctiveness, and Jewish refusal to dine with non-Jews was regarded as antisocial by some ancient authors (Acts 10:28; 11:3; Tacitus *Hist.* 5.5; Josephus *Ag. Ap.* 2.148, 258; Philostratus *Vit. Apoll.* 5.33). It is unsurprising, then, that given the Jewish context of early Christianity, the major debates in the early church were over food and fellowship (see Gal 2:11–14; Acts 10:14; Rom 14; 1 Cor 8). Abstention from **drink** probably concerns wine consumed as part of libations to the gods, which meant that it was contaminated by idolatry (Dan 1:3–16; 10:3; Add Esth 14:17; *Jos. Asen.* 8:5; *m. 'Abod. Zar.* 2:3; 5:2; cf. 1 Cor 10:31; Rom 14:17), or else because liquids were thought to be susceptible to impurity (e.g., CD 12:15–17; *m. Ber.* 8:2). The **feast** could designate Jewish festivals such as Passover, Tabernacles, or Pentecost. The **New Moon** is slightly more ambiguous as it was deemed to have significance for a number of religious groups and philosophies, but given what precedes a connection with the Jewish cultus is most likely (Num 10:10; 2 Kgs 4:23; Ps 81:3; Isa 1:13; Ezek 46:3, 6). We seem to have here fairly definitive evidence for the Jewish nature of the philosophy since, socially speaking, it required the observance of customs that demarcated the Jewish people in a pagan environment. The underlying assumption is that the Colossians were judged for failing to obey regulations binding upon them, even as Gentiles, if they do not adhere to Jewish practices pertaining to purity laws, Sabbath, and festivals. The implication is that the teachers advocated (partial) adherence to the Torah provides fulness and fulfilment lacking in the Christian message.[30]

The rationale for rejecting the imposition of these Jewish regulations is that they **are merely a shadow of what is to come**. Similar language is used in Heb 10:1 to describe the Old Testament in relation to Christ. This idea draws on the Platonic understanding of the difference between ideal

---

30. As such I reject the view of DeMaris 1994: 51 that there is no polemic against the Mosaic law in Colossians.

and reality, which impacted Hellenistic Judaism since the same concept is found also in Philo.[31] The Torah foreshadows and overtures the Messiah who fulfills the precepts of the law. For Greek-speakers shadows also had negative connotations of instability, shiftiness, weakness, and emptiness (e.g., 1 Chr 29:15; Jas 1:17; Wis 5:9).[32] That the **substance belongs to the Messiah** means that the reality posed by the shadow, and the fulfillment of what is to come, belongs to Jesus. This combines a Platonic idealism with a Jewish eschatology and a focus on Jesus as the goal of Israel's scriptures (see Rom 10:4). The Messiah is the true "substance" of the Torah. Therefore, the law's preparatory adumbrating function has come to an end because the messianic "substance" to which the law pointed has now arrived.[33] This subject relates back to earlier assertions in 1:15–20 where Jesus exercises the prerogative of God as Creator and Reconciler, and 2:9 where the fullness of deity dwells in Jesus. Hence, the incarnation marks the indwelling of God in the body of the Messiah to be among his people.

Paul makes some additional cautionary words with **Let no one disqualify you**, which is a further remark against letting people pass judgment over them. The word for **disqualify** (*katabrabeuō*) can also have the sense of "rob of a prize,"[34] and this sounds like someone trying to throw them out of bounds during a match and eliminate them from a contest (see Gal 5:7). The means through which they might be disqualified is spelled out as giving way to those who insist upon **ascetic practices and worship of angels**. The **ascetic practices** are indicative of humility or self-mortification and probably pertain to fasting (Lev 16:29, 31; 23:27, 32; Num 29:7; Ps 35:13; 69:10; Isa 58:3, 5; Jdt 4:9).[35] Fasting was a precursor

31. Cf. Philo *Conf.* 69; *Flacc.* 165.

32. Gnilka 1980: 147.

33. Beale 2007: 862.

34. BDAG 515.

35. Alternatively, *tapeinophrosunē* could be translated as "humility," and since "humility" and "worship" are governed by the same preposition *en*, it might be translated as the "humility and worship of the angels" and refer to the angels' prostration before God in the act of heavenly worship (see O'Brien 1982: 142; Francis 1975: 180; Rowland 1983: 75; Harris 1991: 121; Sappington 1991: 158–61; Sumney 1993: 376–77; Smith 2006: 130). However, *tapeinophrosunē* is a virtual technical term for fasting in the LXX (Lev 16:29, 31 etc.) and early Christian literature (e.g., Tertullian *Jejun.* 12, *Herm. Vis.* 3.10.6; 5.3.7). In Col 2:23 *tapeinophrosun tē* is linked with asceticism and the positive virtue of humility in Col 3:12 (cf. Stettler 2005: 183). Arnold (1996: 53 [see also pp. 210–14]) points out that in the *Sepher Ha-Razim* ("Book of Mysteries," a collection of Jewish incantation texts) the intercession of angels depends upon ritual purity.

to visionary experiences, angelic visitations, and heavenly ascents. Fasting leading to ecstatic states may have enabled participants to have, or claim to have had, visions of angelic worship (e.g., Dan 10:2–3; *4 Ezra* 5:13, 20; *Gk. Apoc. Ezra* 1:2–7). The worship in question could be worship directed *towards* the angels,[36] but more likely worship *with* the angels.[37] The notion of sharing in the worship offered by angels is part of the great tradition of Jewish visionary revelations (e.g., Isa 6:2–3; Dan 7:10; Luke 2:14; and Rev 4–5). The evidence from Qumran suggests that worship with angels was much coveted, and the Qumranites' own liturgies were thought to include the presence of the angels (e.g., 1QH 3:21–22; 11:10–13; 1QM 7:4–6; 1QSa 2:8–9; 1QSb 4:25–26). A plausible scenario, then, is that the teachers propagated the necessity of ascetic practices leading to visions of the angelic praises of heaven. This was a means to assuaging, pleasing, or submitting to the "rulers and authorities" who exercised some form of influence over them. This line of argument seems justified in light of the following statement that the persons urging them to go down this line describe in detail things **which he has purportedly seen on entering (heaven),[38] vainly being puffed up by his fleshly mind.** What is at stake is not only the claim to possess special access to the operation of heavenly liturgy, but the status and prestige that these visions afford to their participants. The teachers are also seers, and their accounts of visions combined with the prowess of their instruction invest them with a special authority, rather like the "spiritual ones" (*pneumatikoi*) in First Corinthians (3:1;

36. On the worship of angels in Asia Minor see DeMaris 1994: 62; Arnold 1996: 8–102. Prohibition of angel worship is frequent in various Jewish and Christian writings, e.g., Deut 4:19; 17:3; Jer 8:2; 19:13; Zeph 1:5; *Apoc. Zeph.* 6:15; *Apoc. Ab.* 17:2; *Ascen. Isa.* 7:21; Rev 19:10; 22:9.

37. Cf. Francis 1975: 176–81; against this interpretation see Lohse 1971: 118–19; Arnold 1996: 90–95; Lincoln 2000: 563–64.

38. The Greek here is notoriously obscure (esp. the antecedent of the neuter relative pronoun *ha* [see BDF § 154]). The meaning of the word *embateutō* is open to debate, and some have translated it "entering into," which could be related to initiation rites in the mystery cults (e.g., Lohse 1971: 119–21) or "going into detail about" some object of interest (see H. Preisker, *TDNT* 2:535–36; BDAG 321; TNIV). The evidence for the use of the term in mystery initiations is a century later than Colossians and the word was frequent in Jewish apocalyptic literature in reference to visionary ascents (Francis 1975: 172–75; Rowland 1983: 75–76). Most likely *embateutō* has connotations of entering deeply into a subject (2 Macc 2:30; Philo *Plant.* 80). Thus, at this point it probably means the descriptive report coming from someone who has claimed to enter into heaven (see N. Walter, *EDNT* 1:442). See further Evans 1982: 196–98; Sappington 1991: 155–58; Harris 1991: 121–22; Smith 2006: 127–30.

14:37). The visions are not a means to edify others, but become a vehicle for pressing one's own claim to worth and value in a religious association. Paul can speak of his own visionary experiences (2 Cor 12:2–7), but he did not see it as a means of boasting or self-promotion, which is the exact opposite of those who are **puffed up**. The teachers become self-inflated, conceited (on *physioō* see 1 Cor 4:6, 18–19; 5:2; 8:1; 13:4), and possess a **fleshly mind** driven by the carnality of human existence as opposed to a mind nurtured by the praises of the heavenlies as is claimed.

A further polemical description pertains to those who are not **grasping the head**. Here **head** is an obvious reference to Jesus (1:18; 2:10), but the failure to grasp Jesus Christ could lie with one or more groups. This could conceivably mean that some believers in Colossae, already influenced by the philosophy, fail to comprehend the full account of their riches in Messiah and fail to apprehend the fullness of God in the Messiah. Or else, and more probable, it signifies that the teachers external to the community simply do not "get it," or do not register the reality of Jesus's identity and authority.[39] Paul proceeds to use a body metaphor (see Rom 12:4; 1 Cor 12:12–31) to refer to Jesus as the one **from whom** the body is nourished and united together. The quest for a maturity and **growth** that comes from God is ultimately attained only in the Messiah.

Paul briefly recaps the nature of his discourse so far. Whereas he has moved largely from the indicative (i.e., burial and resurrection with the Messiah, vv. 8–15) to the imperative (i.e., do not surrender your freedom, vv. 16–18), he works here from the indicative to an interrogative in order to press his point with greater rhetorical effect. The conditional clause **if you died with the Messiah** expresses the reality of vv. 12–13 and not doubt.[40] The **elemental forces** are the hostile angelic beings of the heavenly realm, which, as made known in 2:15, Jesus has gloriously triumphed over. Yet if this is the case, Paul legitimately asks, **why, as if you were living in the world, do you continue to submit to its regulations?** This is the first clear instance that the philosophy has made some headway into

---

39. Barth and Blanke (1994: 385–87) suppose that the teachers represent persons who are outside of the Colossian community, but nonetheless perceive themselves as Christians with an exclusively elitist self-concept, which is expressed in various Jewish ordinances and which they are attempting to make obligatory for the church in general. For me that description corresponds more closely to the opponents in Galatians rather than in Colossians.

40. Cf. BDF § 373.

the Colossian community and this action is inconsistent with the pattern of teaching that they have received. The **regulations** in question relate primarily to abstinence, separation, and the maintenance of purity, which are typical concerns of Jewish communities living in pagan majority environments. Hence, the triadic commandments which Paul derides: **do not handle, do not taste, do not touch**, and this may be a slogan of the teachers in Colossae themselves that Paul negatively repeats. The **regulations** (see 2:14) are described as **commandments**, which Paul uses to describe the Torah elsewhere (e.g., Rom 7:8–13), and as **teachings of men**, which most likely denotes interpretation and application of the Torah.[41] In other words, in an argument very much akin to Gal 4:8–10, Paul is saying that submission to Torah + mysticism involving angels means being in bondage to powers opposed to human beings. The Torah may have been given to Moses by angels (Gal 3:19), but obeying it will not appease the angels as much as enslave believers to them. Just as they died to the law (Gal 2:19; Rom 7:4) so too they have died to the angelic beings who gave it. Subservience to angelic powers is singularly inappropriate because the Colossians themselves are raised and seated with Messiah (2:12; 3:1–2) and, in a particular sense, are not **living in this world**. Furthermore, in a side remark, Paul says that these restrictive regulations are themselves unimportant because they **perish as they are used up**, and so, the material things of the world become immaterial in light of the cross and resurrection. Thus, Paul counters a theology of purity and pollution with one of new creation and the cross. Paul counters a philosophy with Platonic overtones by using a Platonic argument about the difference between ideal and reality rooted in a theology of the incarnation and a redemptive historical scheme of promise and fulfillment.

In a further remark, Paul states that the philosophy of the teachers may have an outward appearance of providing a path to **wisdom**, but in reality, it is a form of **pseudo-piety** or "man-made religion" (see "self-made religion" [ESV, NASB]; "self-imposed worship" [NIV]; "self-imposed piety" [NRSV]). The mandated **ascetic practices** and **harsh treatment of the body**, acts of self-deprivation, do not attain the goals to which they reportedly claim and thus have no **value**. For Paul, **restraining the gratifications of the flesh** is not achieved by Torah, which antagonizes rather than

41. The words "commandments" (*entalamata*) and "teachings" (*didaskalia*) are also found in Matt 15:9, Mark 7:7, and Isa 29:13 LXX.

solves the Adamic condition of humanity (see Rom 5:20).[42] Of course, as Paul addresses in Roman 6 and Galatians 5, if obedience to Torah and its various commandments is no longer the definitive charter and code of conduct for God's people, then how does one prevent converted pagans from reverting back to their old idolatrous and immoral ways? The answer is not by imposing Torah on them; rather, it is the teaching of Jesus, the example of Jesus, and life in the Spirit.[43] These remarks might seem like terse comments about freedom from certain rules, but they go far beyond that. It is about the goodness and grace of the body. Debates about the body, escaping it or beating it into submission, are the tip of the iceberg for theological debates about the nature of creation and salvation.

Fusing the Horizons: Common Faith

The new covenant community has always been a creedal community confessing its faith as to what God has done in creation, in the history of Israel, in Jesus, and in the life of the church. The triune God has made himself known in his acts of reconciliation and renewal, and this fills the content of sermons, Bible studies, liturgies, songs, prayers, creeds, and confessions from ancient times until even now. For this reason, the early church developed creeds as short programmatic summaries of its faith. These creeds enabled the church to know its own mind and to state how it distinguished itself from Judaism and paganism and from unwholesome derivations of its own beliefs. While no one likes people who are doctrinaire and unduly infatuated with doctrinal precision over every minor issue, nonetheless, we cannot help but notice that the content of faith matters immensely. A common faith is what ultimately defines the center and boundaries of the church and even forms the fulcrum of our common fellowship.

It is vitally important, then, that the church in all ages guard its theological vision of the nature of God, Christ, and salvation without being pointlessly puritanical or vacuously broad. Even though it might seem unpopular, we should maintain the language of "heresy" and warnings against it. Since perversions of our distinct theological vision can endanger the integrity of our

42. Cf. Lightfoot 1879: 204–6; Moule 1957: 108–10; Wright 1986: 128; MacDonald 2008: 118.

43. Cf. Bird 2008a: 134–49.

message, the focus of our worship, detract from our mission, and even risk shipwrecking our faith upon the jagged rocks of cultural conformity. Heretics never claim to distort the biblical and ancient faith, but to make it more palatable and pliable to the spirit of the age, and so remove barriers to belief. For the second-century Gnostics this meant marrying Christianity to Platonic cosmology, and for the old liberals of the early twentieth century it required revising Christian doctrines in light of rationalistic critiques of revealed religion. We should embody the virtue of tolerance, especially in matters that are *adiaphora* or "indifferent," but at the same time we should think carefully of what we tolerate and not allow anyone to bring sin or false teaching into the church and expect it to be baptized and blessed in Jesus's name.

We live in an age where, in some circles, inclusiveness has become the new orthodoxy and exclusiveness is the only heresy. This is where Col 2:8–23 is so important. It informs us that some things are not for negotiation, such as the sufficiency and supremacy of Christ, and that nothing can supplement God's actions in his anointed Son. Colossians demands no compromise to the creed of *solus Christus* or "Christ alone." To capitulate this point will result in a theology that is at first imprecise, then wishy-washy, then populist, then worldly, and finally trivial. Paul calls on Christian communities to confess their faith with courage and fidelity against the philosophies of this world, be they within the church or external to it, and to singularly propound without reservation the absolute finality and ultimacy of Jesus Christ in all things. From this faithful confession emerges a unity rooted in one faith, one Lord, and one baptism; it unites believers from all over the world, it brings them together in a common mission, it entreats them to recline at a common table, and forges their shared identity as those who are in the Messiah.

Excursus: Colossians and the Roman Empire

In recent Pauline studies a growing number of researchers have been paying attention to the political background of Paul's letters. This involves looking at how a number of his favored terms like "gospel," "Lord," "Savior," "citizenship," "*parousia*," and "kingdom" are mirrored in the Roman sociopolitical sphere. It is accompanied by examination of Roman propaganda and the imperial cult of emperor worship as the foil for much of Paul's theology. Commentators then posit elements of counter-imperial theology in Paul's letters, which amount to a veiled protest against the social order, military power, and political tyranny of the Roman Empire. This has even been dubbed the "Fresh Perspective on Paul" by N. T. Wright.[44] We should be cautious of this approach in so far that it can seem a little too congenial to fashionable anti-Americanism (where America is the new "Rome"). It potentially mistakes context for content, and this perspective often does some scandalously creative exegesis of Rom 13:1–8 where Paul urges believers to submit to state authorities. Paul was not a white, suburban, middle-class, liberal arts teacher, educated in the 1960s, and neither does every reference to Jesus as *Kurios* ("Lord") automatically demand the antiphon, "and Caesar is not."[45] Yet there can be no denying the theopolitical dimension to Paul's theology and the counter-imperial implications of much of his thought.[46] If, as tradition tells us, Paul was executed in Rome, it was not because he practiced some kind of interiorized spirituality to the effect that "Jesus is Lord of my heart," but something of his message and conduct brought him to the attention of the imperial authorities and warranted capital punishment in their eyes. We should also remember that opposition to the politics and pantheon of the pagan nations was at the very root of Israel's exclusive devotion to Yahweh, as the nations would one day be in submission to the God of Israel, the God of the Jews. This is why Jews, generally speaking, sought exemption from service in the Roman army and why some zealous-minded Galileans had as their motto "no king but God."[47] Judea was the only nation that refused to engage in a god swap with Rome, whereby both groups added the other's gods to their pantheon of deities and prescribed rituals that paid homage to both groups of gods. The angry mob who dragged Paul's friends before the city authorities in Thessalonica understood the potentially subversive nature of this Jesus movement when they said of Christians, "These men who have caused trouble all over the world have now come here, and Jason has welcomed them into his house. They are all defying Caesar's decrees, saying that there is another king, one called Jesus" (Acts 17:6–7 TNIV). The first Christians were not political activists, but neither did they possess a spirituality detached from political realities, for the final consummation of the kingdom of God would spell the end of all human domains of authority opposed to God's reign on earth.

44. Wright 2005: 59–79.

45. For criticisms of this "Fresh Perspective" see, e.g., Burk 2008 and Kim 2008.

46. For overviews see Gorman 2004, 117–13; Bird 2008a, 83–90.

47. Josephus *Ant.* 14.228, 232; 18.23.

It is possible to identify a number of elements in Paul's letter to the Colossians that carry theopolitical implications and perhaps make a tacit jibe against Roman imperial claims if we read the literary subtext and social context carefully.[48] (1) We have already seen that the language of Jesus as possessing "preeminence" in 1:18 might call to mind the image of the Roman emperor as *auctoritas*, that is, the one possessing an unsurpassable degree of power and prestige. It could well be that "Lord Jesus Christ" (1:3; cf. 2:6) corresponds to the Roman emperors' throne name, "Imperator Caesar Augustus" or "Imperator Nero Augustus."[49] (2) The celebrated and deified *pax Romana* (peace of Rome) that was created by imperial violence is eclipsed by the "peace of Messiah" (3:15), which results in reconciliation brought about by Jesus's sacrificial death (1:15–23). (3) Jesus's death is treated as a Roman triumph over rebellious subjects (2:15) and the metaphor clearly mimics and mocks Roman victory celebrations. Disarming, crucifying, and basking in bloody glory is what the Romans did, except that here the roles seem to be reversed and the victim has become the victor. (4) The incorporation of trans-ethnic identities like Jew, Gentile, Barbarian, and Scythian into "Messiah" mirrors the attempt of Rome to incorporate peoples and kingdoms into its empire by granting citizenship and benefaction to conquered territories. (5) The "gospel" (1:5, 23) mirrors imperial statements that celebrate the good news of the emperor's birth and accession. The gospel of Rome grew and spread with its successful campaigns and the gospel of Paul grew with its Spirit driven proclamation and reception. The question is: "Whose gospel is the source of a fruitfulness that will last and sustain the world—the gospel of Caesar or the gospel of Jesus?"[50] (6) The hostile powers that Jesus subjugates may include deceased Roman emperors who were thought to become gods after death (i.e., apotheosis) or even living emperors. Nero's example might be particularly relevant assuming a date for Colossians in the late 50s or early 60s. Nero was acclaimed as "Jupiter himself on earth in altered guise, or one other of the powers above concealed under an assumed mortal semblance" (1:16; 2:8, 15, 20).[51] I doubt that Colossians was written or heard as a counter-imperial manifesto, but the content and context of the imagery does naturally lend itself to contrasting two metanarratives about the salvation of

48. Cf. Walsh and Keesmaat 2004; Maier 2005.

49. Richard 1988, 326.

50. Walsh and Keesmaat 2004: 75.

51. Calpurnius Siculus *Ecl.* 4.142–46 (cited in Maier 2005: 337). On the Roman Empire as one of the many "powers" see Walsh and Keesmaat 2004: 91–92.

the world. Would "salvation" come via the semi-divine emperor conquering and civilizing remote kingdoms, or through God-in-Messiah restoring Israel and rescuing the nations from the mire of sin and death? If Paul and his co-workers believed that the "kingdom of the son of his love" was both an alternative to and eventual replacement for the Roman Empire, then we cannot help but see in Colossians a thinly veiled protest against the power and propaganda of the Roman state.

TRANSFORMED AND RENEWED:
New Creation and the New Life (3:1–17)

¹ If then you have been raised with Messiah, seek the things above where Messiah is, enthroned at the right hand of God. ² Set your minds on the things above and not on the things of earth. ³ For you have died and your life has been hidden with Messiah in God. ⁴ When Messiah, who is your life, is manifested, then you also will be manifested with him in glory.

⁵ Therefore, put to death the members of your earthly being, sexual immorality, impurity, lust, evil desires, and greed, which is idolatry. ⁶ Because of which the wrath of God is coming upon the sons of disobedience ⁷ and you formerly walked in them when you lived in these things. ⁸ But now you must also put off all such things, anger, wrath, malice, slander, and perverse talk from your mouth. ⁹ Do not lie to one another, (because you) have stripped off the old man with its deeds ¹⁰ and having clothed yourselves with the new man, which is being renewed according to the image of the one creating him. ¹¹ In that renewal there is no longer Greek and Jew, circumcised and uncircumcised, Barbarian, Scythian, slave, and free; but Messiah is for all and in all.

¹² Therefore, as God's elect, holy and beloved, clothe yourselves with hearts of compassion, kindness, humility, meekness, and patience. ¹³ Bearing with one another, and if anyone has a complaint against someone, forgive each other just as the Lord graciously forgave you, and thus so with you too. ¹⁴ And to all these virtues add love, which is the bond of perfect unity. ¹⁵ And let the peace of Messiah arbitrate in your hearts, into which you were called in one body—and so be thankful. ¹⁶ Let the word of Messiah dwell in you richly,

teaching and admonishing each other in all wisdom, singing psalms, hymns, and spiritual songs with thanksgiving in your hearts to God. [17] And whatever you do, in word or deed, do all things in the name of the Lord Jesus, giving thanks to God the Father through him.

The material in 3:1–17 is a distinct unit that is premised on the reality of union with Messiah and the various imperatives that such a union creates for the individual believer and for the new covenant community. This provides a natural progression from the preceding section in 2:8–23, where Paul has argued that the Colossians are not indebted to the hybrid Hellenism and Jewish mysticism of the teachers with their system of heavenly intermediaries, asceticism, and coercive practice of Torah observances. Paul is advocating a competing moral vision to the constraining tendencies of the teachers.[1] Additionally, Paul is pointing out that freedom from Torah does not mean freedom from any kind of moral obligation. As Paul does elsewhere, such as in Romans (6:1–23; 7:1–6; 8:1–16; 12:1–2) and Galatians (5:13–6:10), he follows up his theological explication of the message of salvation with a behavioral discourse concerning the way that believers and the communities that they constitute are to live in view of so great a salvation. This is known generally as the *indicative* and the *imperative* of Pauline ethics—because you are united with Messiah you are no longer to offer your bodies to the service of sin. As believers live between the triumph of Christ's death and the manifestation of his glory at his Parousia, they struggle against the flesh and the powers in the time in between. Thus, the bulk of the material in 3:1–17 functions rhetorically as an exhortation focusing on the transformative nature of the gospel as they live between the ages. Paul's gospel is transformative in the sense of firstly transporting believers from darkness to light (Col 1:13–14) and from death to life (Col 3:3–4), and secondly by giving them a new identity in Jesus Christ (Col 2:6–7, 11; 3:11). Charles Moule put it well: "Thus, the new life is a *fait accompli* because of Christ: it is a free gift

---

1. On a link between the exhortation in Col 3:1—4:6 and the argument against the teachers in 2:6–23, see also Sappington 1991: 143; Wall 1993: 129; Hartman 1995: 189–90; Dunn 1996: 199–201; McL. Wilson 2005: 234; Smith 2006: 172–74 in contrast to Barth and Blanke 1994: 391–92.

from God; but it carries a challenge. If we accept that challenge, we begin to belong to the final event, to God's ultimate purpose: we have entered into the new covenant . . . But the process of fully becoming detached from the old and fully belonging to the new remains to be painfully and laboriously completed."[2]

Importantly, 3:1–17 does not constitute an insertion of general Christian paranesis or moral exhortation into this segment of the letter independent of the literary context. There is an indelible link to what has gone before.[3] The imagery of 3:1 picks up the theme of Christ's resurrection and triumph in 2:10, 12, 15 and lordship in 1:15–20. The reference to death in 3:3 echoes 2:12, 20 where death with the Messiah abounds in liberation from all forms of evil. The virtue of humility in 3:12 contrasts naturally with the false humility of the teachers in 2:18, 23. The apocalyptic motif of 3:3–4 rehearses Paul's earlier remarks in 1:26–27 and 2:2–3 about mystery/hidden things being revealed. Paul is returning to a theme in the introduction of this epistle, where his prayer was that the Colossians would "walk worthily of the Lord in order to fully please him, bearing fruit in every good work and growing in the knowledge of God" (1:10). Paul intends the Colossians to be completely renewed in their understanding of God and morally transformed in regards to their lives, producing God-pleasing behavior. Fundamental to the exhortation in this section is *taxis* or "ordering" one's life according to the symbol of baptism where one has died and risen with Christ (2:5, 11–12; 3:1) and according to the new creation which brings believers into the new age and renders null and void their ethnic and gender distinctions in the economy of salvation (3:11). It is also about implementing the "word of Messiah," which is the pattern of teaching *from* the Messiah and *about* the Messiah (3:16). This in turn generates a new *praxis* that transforms one's ethics, speech, values, relationships, attitudes, actions, and worldview. The new covenant community is one that embodies and fulfills the highest moral ideals of the Torah but owes its energy and impetus to Jesus and not to the letter of the law. In keeping with the central thesis or rhetorical *propositio* of Col 1:15–20, the exhortation is highly christocentric.[4] Paul prescribes

2. Moule 1973: 483.

3. So also Hendriksen 1964: 139; Lohse 1971: 132; O'Brien 1982: 158; Barth and Blanke 1994: 391; Dunn 1996: 200; Thompson 2005: 69; McL. Wilson 2005: 234; and more cautiously Martin 1973: 100.

4. Harris 1991: 136; Dunn 1996: 200.

an ethical paradigm for the Colossians that finds its imperative neither in playing on their old pagan superstitious fears nor by foisting on them the Mosaic code, but apprehends righteousness and holiness from the power of renewal working in them because Messiah dwells in them.

THE BASIS OF THE NEW LIFE:
UNION WITH THE RISEN AND EXALTED MESSIAH (3:1–4)

It is possible to take Col 3:1–4 as a transitional section that summarizes the argument in 2:9–23 while also looking forward to the exhortation of 3:5—4:6.[5] In vv. 1–4 Paul urges the Colossians to understand their very own identities as being bound up with Jesus Christ, and this most naturally lends itself to seeking and setting their minds on the things above where Christ is seated and not orienting themselves towards earthly things. Paul premises this argument with the statement about participation in Christ's resurrection and death. He says, **if then you have been raised with Messiah**, which grammatically is posed in such a way that the circumstances are assumed to be true.[6] They have been raised with Messiah and this impacts the thought life and values of the Colossian Christians.[7] The accompanying commands **seek** and **set your mind** upon the **things above** is not pietistic escapism but refers to a steadfast devotion to Jesus Christ which determines the attitudes of the believer. The **things above** stand for the hope of the gospel (1:5), the invisible God (1:15),

5. Wolter (1993: 164–65) identifies Col 3:1–4 as a *peroratio* and recapitulating the *argumentatio* of Col 2:9–23 and preparing for the *exhortatio* in Col 3:5–4:6. Cf. also O'Brien 1982: 157–58 for the looking backward and forward function of this section.

6. Abbott 1897: 278; Martin 1973: 100; O'Brien 1982: 158; Wright 1986: 131; Barth and Blanke 1994: 392; Garland 1998: 201. For a similar strategy see Phil 2:1–4 where Paul uses the same if/since style of argument in aid of ethical exhortation.

7. Elsewhere Paul speaks of being crucified with Christ (Gal 2:20; Rom 6:6), died/baptized/buried with Christ (Rom 6:3–5), but he only ever speaks of being raised with Christ in the future tense (Rom 6:5). Several scholars seize on this and argue that the author of Colossians and Ephesians has collapsed the eschatological future, the "not-yet" into the present and have essentially a wholly realized eschatology. A number of things count against this view (see the introduction as well): (1) The "not-yet" or unrealized aspect of the salvation experience is very much on the fore of Colossians as is evident from 3:3–4, 10, 24–25, and 4:2. (2) Dunn (1996: 201) is right when he states that this section "maintains a characteristically Pauline balance between teaching and parenesis, 'already and 'not yet,' heavenly perspective and everyday responsibility." See also McL. Wilson (2005: 236, 240, 252) who thinks the author exceeds Paul but remains true to Paul's overall eschatological perspective.

and the reign of Jesus over the cosmos (2:8). These heavenly things are opposed to the things below, which are the philosophy, human traditions, the flesh, elemental forces, and human made religious asceticism (2:8, 11, 13, 15, 16–18, 22–23). In the new self that they are to be clothed in, the Colossians are to embody the things of heaven and manifest those virtues that reflect the life of Jesus Christ in their renewed existence.[8] What is more, because the Messiah has been **enthroned** at the right hand of God (see Ps 110:1, the most cited OT passage in the NT) he possesses all authority, majesty, and power, and naturally one looks to him as the source and sustainer of authentic Christian life.[9] The messianic promise that God would exalt and honor the anointed one of Israel is fulfilled in Jesus's resurrection and ascension. As a consequence, the community looks to Jesus as the Messiah whom God has exalted high above all earthly potentates and powers. To use a paraphrase: "Set your hearts on and allow your imagination to be liberated to comprehend Christ's legitimate rule."[10] By virtue of looking to Messiah, the community of faith is linked to the heavenly world and clings to him so that they might be free from that which would draw them downwards.[11] As Jesus is installed with authority and power, no principality can prevent access to him, nor can any ascetic tradition enhance the human capacity to enter into his presence, since the initiative for salvation resides in God who transferred believers from darkness to the kingdom of his Son (Col 1:13) and reconciled them to himself (Col 1:20). Whereas the Stoics could urge people to seek the heavenly utopia or to apply heavenly perspectives to their earthly life, for Paul seeking heavenly things requires seeking the Messiah.[12] Thus, for Paul a heavenly perspective on things will mean a Christ-centered perspective. The fullness of the heavens that the teachers wish to lead the Colossians to stands in contrast to Paul's Messiah who is seated far above all angels and intermediaries and rules heaven as God's vice-regent.

The second "indicative" aspect is **for you have died, and your life has been hidden with Messiah in God**, and this signifies the destruction

8. Foster 2008, 115–16.

9. On the apostolic preaching of the ascension see Acts 2:33–35; 5:31; 7:55–56; Rom 8:34; Eph 1:20; Heb 1:3, 13; 8:1; 10:12; 12:2; 1 Pet 3:22; Rev 3:21.

10. Walsh and Keesmaat 2004: 155.

11. Lohse 1971: 133.

12. Engberg-Pedersen (2000: 90–100) finds a Stoic background of a similar order in Philippians 3 amidst Paul's notion of a heavenly citizenship.

of their old *id*entities through the cross. The aorist verb *apethanete* (**you died**) points back to baptism-confession as the moment of identifying with Christ's death and resurrection. The **life that is hidden with Messiah in God** stands for the structure of their existence. It is a life that is lived out in the world through an exterior resource (Rom 6:4; 2 Cor 4:10–11; 13:4). Such a life has its center with Christ in God (Phil 1:21). It is lived for God and his Messiah (Rom 6:10–11; 14:8; 2 Cor 5:15) and continues on under the aegis of the faithfulness of the Son of God (Gal 2:19–20).[13] Paul's apocalyptic orientation shines through in v. 4 as he tells the Colossians that **when Messiah is manifested** then they **will be manifested with him in glory**. This is the only point in Colossians where Paul alludes to Christ's *parousia* or second advent. The manifestation or revealing of Christ at the *parousia* will disclose the reality of these believers. It will show that they are "of Messiah" and it will also evince the true character of their lives as being soaked in and pervaded by Jesus Christ's own life. The glory in particular may be associated with the resurrection of believers (see 1 Cor 15:42–43; Phil 3:20–21; 2 Thess 2:14). The believer's life in Christ then can be sketched in three stages: (1) they have died and risen with Jesus, (2) their present life is hidden with Messiah, and (3) at his coming they will be revealed in glory.[14] When once asked if he was "saved," B. F. Westcott replied: "I am saved, I am being saved, I will be saved" (see 2 Cor 1:9–10). By identifying with Messiah in heaven, the Colossians participate in the fruits of salvation and also anticipate the consummation of that salvation at the revelation of the Messiah.[15]

LIVING AS THE NEW HUMANITY OF THE NEW AGE (3:5–11)

The inference that Paul draws (**Therefore**) in v. 5 is that if they have died with Messiah then they must enact this death and **put to death the members of your earthly being**. That carries the sense of killing, murdering, or destroying the earthly nature which stands as the antithesis to the Christ-saturated life which they now partake of (see Rom 6:11; 8:13). One is either dead in sin (Col 2:13) or dead to sin (Col 3:5).[16] The

13. Dunn 1996: 207.
14. Thompson 2005: 69.
15. Keck 1988: 78.
16. Garland 1998: 203.

teachers wish to impose partial Torah observance on the Colossians in order to restrain their fleshly desires (what the Rabbis called the *yetzer hara* or "evil impulse"). That is tantamount to putting the wild animals of lust, hatred, and greed into cages where they remain alive and continue to be a dangerous threat to their captors. Paul's solution is more radical: the animals need to be killed.[17] The command **put to death** can be related to similar commands in v. 8, **put off/strip off**, with a net affect of doing away with such behaviors. The phrasing in relation to **earthly** is awkward and can be interpreted differently (e.g., "mundane ordinances" [Lightfoot], "whatever in you is earthly" [NRSV], "whatever in your nature belongs to the earth" [NET], "things used for earthly purposes" [Harris], "earthly things lurking within you" [NLT]).[18] But the point is to allow a heavenly perspective to determine one's being rather than allowing an earthbound perspective to shape one's behavior. What that means is underscored with the following vice list in which Paul urges them to put to death certain activities and attitudes: **sexual immorality, impurity, lust, evil desires, and greed which is idolatry**. Vice lists are common in both Paul's letters and in Jewish and Greco-Roman literature.[19] Its function here is to provide real content to activities and attitudes that are proscribed. Further explanation is given is v. 7: **because of which the wrath of God is coming upon the sons of disobedience**. The avoidance of such vices is not only because they adversely affect the domains of horizontal (human–human) and vertical (human–divine) relationships, but because such things occasion the **wrath of God**. Wrath (*orgē*) is understood here not in the sense of God's capacity for unbridled violence, but as the righteous indignation of God's holiness towards moral evil.[20] For Paul, God's wrath is something that comes as a result of God's character and due to the eschatological trajectory that will see all wickedness subdued and punished by the inescapable justice of God (see Rom 1:18; 2:5; 1 Thess 2:16). Because of Jesus's

17. Wright 1986: 128.

18. The meaning depends on whether the word *gēs* ("earth") is taken as a substantive adjective "earthly" or as a noun "earth."

19. Cf. e.g., Wis 14:25–26; 4 Macc 1:26–27; 2:15; 1QS 4:9–11; 2 *En.* 10:4–5. If some think that Paul's vice lists are needless long and detailed then I urge a comparison with the vice lists compiled by Philo *Sacr.* 32, which includes 150 prohibited vices and behaviours. Paul's lists are meager in comparison.

20. As McL. Wilson (2005: 247) puts it, God "is not a benign old gentleman over whose eyes the wool may be pulled with impunity, a god whose only function is to forgive."

death, believers are delivered from God's wrath (Rom 5:9; 1 Thess 1:10; 5:9) since Jesus has propitiated God's wrath with such finality and with such perfection that none remains for them (Rom 3:25).[21] The objects of wrath are described as **sons of disobedience**, which, though textually questionable,[22] may be taken as a euphemism for sons of perdition (see John 17:12) and reflects the Hebrew idiom that a son's conduct reflects his paternal origins. The relevance of this description of human depravity is that **you formerly walked in them when you lived in these things**, and Paul (as he does elsewhere, e.g., Col 1:21 and 1 Cor 1:26–31; 6:9–11; 12:2; Gal 4:8–9; Eph 2:1–3) poses a sharp contrast between what the believers were before Messiah and what they are now in Messiah. Those that **walked** and **lived** in such disobedience experienced the depersonalizing effects of sin and alienation from the Creator (see Rom 1:18–32).

The temporal contrast gives way to a logical contrast with **but now**, which echoes Paul's eschatological "now" that marks the coming of the new age in the Messiah (cf. Col 1:22; Eph 2:13; Rom 3:21). What the Colossians are to do in order to further the transition from their former life to their new life in Messiah is to **put off all such things**. This leads to another vice list that can be grouped into sins of aggression (**anger, wrath, malice**) and sins of the tongue (**slander, perverse talk, lie to one another**). What makes this a possibility that Paul expects to be realized is not a more stringent and concerted application of the moral will, but rather the power and glory of the new creation spilling over into their lives. This is verbalized with **have stripped off the old man with its deeds and having clothed yourselves with the new man which is being renewed according to the image of the one creating him**. The aorist participles (*apekdusamenoi*, **stripped off**; *endusamenoi*, **having clothed**) probably hark back to their baptism (Col 3:1) as the point in which they first put on Messiah and put off the world (Gal 3:27; cf. Rom 13:14; 1 Pet 5:5). Paul calls on the Colossians to remember their faith, confession, baptism, and the dynamic power that operates in them because it releases them from

---

21. On "wrath" see the helpful discussion in O'Brien 1982: 184–85.

22. The phrase "sons of disobedience" is absent from many textual witnesses (e.g., P[46] D* B Clement Cyprian Ambrosiaster Jerome) and it may have been added by scribes in order to line up with Eph 5:6. Alternatively, the reading before us is contained in a good many witnesses (e.g., ℵ A C D[vid] F G H K L P 33 it vg syr[p] Clement Chrysostom) and v. 7 seems to imply a previous mention of morally reprobate Gentiles, so it may in fact be authentic (Metzger 1994: 557; McL. Wilson 2005: 246).

the power of sin that once dominated them.[23] In contrast to the teachers who advocate asceticism and Torah as the cure to ever returning to pagan revelry, for Paul the power unto a new obedience is the vitalizing grace of God as exerted through the union with the Messiah and as symbolized through the conduit of baptism. It is that faith and initiation into Messiah that has the Colossians being renewed and conformed to the image of God. While echoes of Gen 1:26–27 are quite clear, the verse harks back to what Paul said in Col 1:15, where Jesus is the "image of the invisible God," and Paul also predicates the role of creator to Jesus in Col 1:16. As Jesus Christ is the *icon* of God (Col 1:15; 2 Cor 4:4) so Christians, when Messiah dwells in them, become renewed after the image of God.[24] God's recreation is according to the pattern of Jesus Christ who resembles God's absolute likeness.[25] Jesus is both the *Urmensch* (original man) and *Übermensch* (overcoming man). He is all at once the new Adam, that is, the archetypal pattern of human existence, and simultaneously the triumphant Messiah who reigns as the sovereign Lord over the dominion of God. Hence, this gospel renewal looks back to creation in the pre-fall state of humankind, but also looks forward to the eschaton where believers will be fully conformed to the pattern of Jesus and transformed to reflect the glory of the Messiah (cf. Rom 8:29; 1 Cor 15:49; 2 Cor 3:18; Phil 3:21). Harris offers this paraphrase: "you have stripped off the old Adamic nature, the old humanity, together with the actions that expressed it, and have put on the new nature you have in Christ, the new humanity, which is being renewed day by day in conformity with Christ."[26]

At the mention of the new creation, Paul is unable to restrain his excitement about its implications not only for ethics, but also for identity.

---

23. Martin 1973: 106. Cf. the Westminster Larger Catechism, Question 167: "How is our Baptism to be improved by us?" The answer includes: "by drawing strength from the death and resurrection of Christ, into whom we were baptized, for the mortifying of sin, and quickening of grace, and by endeavouring to live by faith, to have our conservation in holiness and righteousness, as those that have therein given up their names to Christ, and to walk in brotherly love, as being baptized by the same Spirit into one body."

24. On renewal in Paul's letters see 2 Cor 4:16, Rom 12:2, Eph 4:23, and Titus 3:5. On renewal in Pauline theology see especially Buchegger (2003) who contends that in Paul's writings renewal is the process of transformation into the image of God that is realized through the operation of God's glory and via the agency of the Spirit. The concept of renewal is what links together Paul's eschatology, soteriology, and anthropology.

25. Abbott 1897: 284–85; O'Brien 1982: 191.

26. Harris 1991: 155.

He writes that in this **renewal** there is **no longer Greek and Jew, circumcised and uncircumcised, Barbarian, Scythian, slave and free**. Similar to Gal 3:28, Paul is advocating a negation of ethnic and economic realities, in terms of their claims to separation and superiority, by the new creation.[27] It is not that these distinctions cease to exist in some way, but they are now transcended by virtue of the believer's participation in the Messiah. It seems to me that the emphasis in Gal 3:28–29 and Col 3:11 is not the obliteration of different human identities, but the *inclusion* of multiple identities under a single meta-identity ("in Messiah," *en Christō*). But that can only be true if the existing identities, which are a means of distinction and status, are themselves negated in value and lessened in their ability to cause differentiation. The old self is thereby transformed and subsumed beneath a shared meta-identity that can sustain an array of diverse entities within it. So I am a male, but an in-Messiah male; I am a Gentile, but an in-Messiah Gentile. The distinctions of Greek and Jew, or Australian and New Zealander, are enveloped by and subordinated to being *en Christō*.

The subversive nature of Paul's ethics strikes against the jugular of Greco-Roman social stratification with its various tiers of power and privilege. Paul also redefines the boundaries of election in light of the advent of the Messiah. Both the Hellenistic and Jewish spheres knew superiority based on gender, race, and culture. Thales is reported to have given thanks to Fortune that he was born a human being and not a brute, a man and not a woman, a Greek and not a Barbarian.[28] Some of the rabbis practiced a prayer attributed to Rabbi Judah ben El'ai, which said, "Blessed are thou who did not make me Gentile, blessed art thou who did not make me a woman, blessed art thou who did not make me a brute."[29] But no Christian could give thanks for this, nor could they pray this rabbinic prayer. Salvation in Christ completely eliminates any such boasting (see 1 Cor 1:26–31). In the words of the second century Christian apologist Aristides, Christians are a "Third Race," alongside Greeks and Jews (*Apol.* 2).[30] Paul's statement implies a breaking down of the covenant boundaries separating Jew and non-Jew, and, in a sense, expands the currency of

27. Cf. 1 Cor 7:18–19; 12:13; Gal 5:6; 6:15.

28. Diogenes Laertius *Lives of the Philosophers* 1:33.

29. *t. Ber.* 7:18; *y. Ber.* 9:2, 13d; *b. Menah.* 43b.

30. Some manuscripts of Aristides read, "fourth race" and include the designants: Barbarians and Greeks, Jews and Christians.

Israel's election by including Gentiles in its purview. By transforming the inherent value of "Jewishness" and its chief covenant boundary marker of circumcision, Paul was implying that the ethnic and ritual distinctions marking off Jew from Gentile had been removed. Consequently the rationale for separateness from and any sense of superiority over the Gentiles has been nullified by the coming of the Messiah.[31]

The pairing of slave and free denotes the union of persons of diverse social status in the Christian gatherings. While "brotherhood" remained a well-known Hellenistic ideal, the system of patron and client relationships and the values of honor and reciprocation could never really accommodate the union of slave and free. Too much fraternizing with slaves was discouraged since familiarity bred contempt and was bad for discipline. Yet a poignant image of the bond between slave and free is encapsulated in the Christian martyrdom narrative of the Roman matron Perpetua, who stood hand in hand with her slave Felicitas in the arena of Carthage in 202 CE as both women faced a common death for their common faith.[32] Barbarians were the uncultured and primitive tribes looked down upon by the Greeks. Their name is a form of onomatopoeia as their speech sounded to Greeks like they were making incomprehensible mutterings of "bar-bar-bar." Scythians were a race from the area north of the Black Sea and were known for their brutality. Josephus says of them: "Now, as to the Scythians, they take a pleasure in killing men, and differ but little from brute beasts."[33] Yet Paul can include all these groups as part of the new creation (3:10–11) and under the designation "brothers" (1:2). Justin Martyr put it well: "But though a man be a Scythian or a Persian, if he has the knowledge of God and of his Christ, and keeps the everlasting righteous decrees, he is circumcised with the good and beneficial circumcision, and is a friend of God, and God rejoices in his gifts and offerings" (*Dial. Tryph.* 28).

The new creation does not completely negate ethnicity, economics, and gender (Christians continue to be male and female) but those differences are transcended by the glory of the new creation that ebbs into the lives of believers. Thus, the Judaic character of the teachers' instruction

31. Cf. Wright 1986: 139; Dunn 1996: 224–26.

32. *The Acts of Perpetua and Felicitas* cited from Bruce 1957: 277.

33. *Ag. Ap.* 2:269; cf. 2 Macc 4:47; 3 Macc 7:5; 4 Macc 10:7. Understandably several commentators and Bible versions opt for a translation of "savage" to describe the Scythians (Knox 1939: 175; TEV).

is met by Paul's appeal to the unity of Greek and Jew in the Messiah. The esoteric nature of the teachers' instruction is matched by Paul's incorporation of Barbarian and Scythian into the Christian fold.[34] That again cuts at the view that the Colossians should seek either the prestige or protection associated with taking on certain Jewish customs. The new creation fosters a unique bond with Jesus Christ and, by consequence, a unique bond with other Christians (see 2 Cor 5:17; 1 Cor 12:13). Christians are the renewed human race and the new eschatological humanity that model before the world what God had always intended for humans to be: a loving community unified in worship of their Creator. This is followed with a short parenthetical remark that **Messiah is for all and in all**.[35] The grammar is quite awkward, and Paul has expressed similar thoughts elsewhere, though mainly with God as the subject (Rom 11:36; 1 Cor 15:28; Eph 1:23; 4:6). In the Greek text there is no verb "is" between "Messiah" and "all" (lit. "all and in all Messiah"). In light of the preceding text it would seem peculiar to think that Paul is saying that Messiah is Jew and Gentile, circumcision and uncircumcised, etc. The Messiah possesses a relation to the categories of persons just named, but not in the sense of mystically being what they all are at once; more likely, the relation that Messiah has to all races and classes resides in the benefits that his faithfulness, passion, and exaltation confers on each of them. Jesus's death is "for us" (e.g., 1 Thess 5:10; Rom 5:8; and esp. 2 Cor 5:14) and Jesus intercedes "for us" from the heavenly throne room (Rom 8:31–34). Hence, Jesus is *for all* whether Jew or Gentile, slave or free, male or female. Unlike Caesar, Messiah is not *kurios* ("Lord") for the benefit of his own self-aggrandizement, but Lord *for the benefit of others*. In fact, we can also detect in 3:11 some additional counter-imperial whispers. Augustus's *Res gestae* ("things accomplished," cited on his funeral inscription) listed among his exploits a triumphal Roman cosmopolitanism that fulfilled Alexander the Great's incomplete program of bringing the world into trans-ethnic unity based on military conquest, political incorporation, and cultural assimilation.[36] Rather, the basis for a shared unity emerges from a common savior who

34. Lightfoot 1879: 216; Hendriksen 1964: 152; Wall 1993: 144; Dunn 1996: 224.

35. Lightfoot (1879: 219) wrote: "Christ has dispossessed and obliterated all distinctions of religious prerogative and intellectual preeminence and social caste; Christ has substituted Himself for all of these; Christ occupies the whole sphere of human life and permeates all its developments."

36. Maier 2005: 341.

brings salvation not by shedding the blood of his subjects, but instead by shedding his own blood as an atonement for their transgressions (1:14, 20, 22; 2:13; 3:13). In many ways, the whole context of 1:15—4:6 seems set on establishing an alternative set of principles for moral order, self-identity, and future security than that provided by the Roman imperial edifice.

LIVING AS THE NEW ISRAEL IN THE NEW AGE (3:12–17)

Paul steadily moves the train of thought further in v. 12 with **therefore** and identifies the Colossians as **God's elect, holy and beloved**, which are common enough designations for Christians elsewhere in his letters (see Rom 8:33; Titus 1:1). The designation was also a common one for Israel (e.g., Deut 7:6–7; 33:3) and Paul conceives of the church as the representatives of Israel in the messianic age (see Gal 6:16; Phil 3:3). Through faith in Jesus the Colossians are assured of their membership in the people of God, and no addition of distinctive Jewish laws or mystical piety can supplement that. The imperatives of the new creation are reaffirmed, not in the sense of vice lists or proscribed behaviors, but now in a list of virtuous actions and attitudes to be cultivated in the community. They are commanded to **clothe yourselves** or put on qualities including **hearts of compassion, kindness, humility, meekness, and patience** as well as **bearing with one another** and **forgiving each other**. These virtues can be said to represent the *imitatio Christi* ("imitation of Christ") that is coupled with a call to *mutual* understanding and *mutual* forgiveness. Mutuality or reciprocal treatment is emphasized by the pronouns **one another** and **each other**, which are anchored in the example of Jesus Christ, hence the clause **just as the Lord graciously forgave you**. Paul calls on them not only to remember this forgiveness, but to replicate it among themselves. There are undoubtedly some echoes of the Jesus tradition here, where Jesus commanded his followers to forgive each other in an almost scandalous way (e.g., Luke 11:4/Matt 6:12, 14–15; Luke 17:4/Matt 18:21–22; Matt 18:23–35; Luke 23:34; John 20:23). For Jesus as for Paul, to be part of the new Israel entails that the Colossians show their family likeness by imparting what they have already received themselves: forgiveness.[37] The realization that each person in their midst is still in the process of

---

37. Lucas 1980: 151.

renewal means that forgiveness is essential for the functioning of the new humanity that the new Israel is called to be.[38] The language of forgiveness is drawn from the world of human relationships: the journey from anguish to restoration. Forgiveness does not mean that one ceases to feel the hurt and pain associated with someone's failing, but it means that one forfeits their right to express their anger, to parade their hurt, and to demand reparation. Forgiveness, as initiated by the wounded party, remains an expression of the divine character and becomes a trait that makes the new covenant community stand out among the cycle of resentment and revenge that typifies human relationships.

A formative conclusion to the moral discourse is contained in the phrase, **And to all these virtues add love, which is the bond of perfect unity**. The preeminence of love in the Christian ethic goes back to Jesus in his combination of the Shema of Deut 6:4–5 with the love command in Lev 19:18 (Matt 22:37–40/Mark 12:30–31/Luke 10:27). According to Paul, love is the surest measure of authentic spirituality (1 Cor 13:1–13). The only thing that counts is faith working through love (Gal 5:6). The love command sums up the whole law (Rom 13:9–10; Gal 5:14). This appeal to love is an important qualification to Paul's rigorous defense of believing integrity (doctrine) and his call for believing uprightness (ethics). Paul is not imparting right doctrine for doctrine's sake, nor is he advocating righteous living for righteousness sake. Instead, he seeks to warn them of the teachers, to conform them to the character of his gospel, and to see them transformed by the power of the Spirit. He seeks to preserve their integrity as Messiah-believing Gentiles and see them in unity with other Gentile Christians, which could be jeopardized if the philosophers win them over. In this sense, warning of potential intruders and admonition against any behavioral lapses are the most loving things one can sometimes do. Love seeks to protect the mind from corruption and keep the soul from perversion by outside forces. Love wants the other in the relationship to live to its fullest potential and to be true to its own identity. Love means seeking to live in wholesome communion within a family of faith, and that is why **love** is the **bond of perfect unity**.

Under a single connective (*kai*, "and") Paul groups two further commands for transformed behavior located around two genitival phrases, the **peace of Messiah** and the **word of Messiah**. Following up the call for

---

38. Lincoln 2000: 650.

love-driven unity is the reference to the **peace of Messiah**, which is a genitive of origin, or the peace that *comes from* Christ, which is to arbitrate in the heart (see John 14:27, "peace I leave with you, my peace I give to you"). Peace seems to have three basic meanings or uses in Paul and all of these are present in Colossians: as a general greeting and blessing along with "grace" (Col 1:2; cf. e.g., Rom 1:7; Gal 1:3; Eph 1:2); as signifying the end of hostilities between God and the believer due to Jesus's death and resurrection (Col 1:20; cf. e.g., Rom 5:1; Eph 2:14–17); and as part of ethical instruction towards good relations and ecclesial unity (Col 3:15; cf. e.g., Rom 12:18; 14:17–19; Gal 5:22; Eph 4:3). The command to let peace arbitrate in the **heart** or permeate one's inner self is made because it is a corollary of being **called** to be part of **one body**. By this Paul probably means to live at peace with other Christians (something he knew much of after painful debates in Antioch, Galatia, and Corinth). Hence there is some justification for adopting the translation **let the peace of Messiah arbitrate in your hearts** in the sense that the peace of Messiah acts as an arbiter when differences between fellow believers arise.[39] The same word (*brabeuō*) occurs in 2:18: "let no one disqualify you" ("be in control of your heart" [NET]; "be umpire" [Lightfoot]). The peace of Messiah acts as an umpire, referee, or arbiter in the community of the new age. By living at peace with fellow Christians, one expresses thankfulness to God for his work in Jesus Christ. To that is added **the word of Messiah**, and the genitive is ambiguous for the reason that it could be an objective genitive (the word *about* Messiah) or else a subjective genitive (the word that *comes from* Messiah). There is no reason to have to choose here, and the word (*logos*) probably denotes all Christian instruction that either derives from the Messiah or has the Messiah as its content and integrating point—what Calvin called "the doctrine of the gospel."[40] The word is meant to **dwell** among them or inhabit their persons. As Wisdom found a dwelling place in Israel (Sir 24:8) and the Spirit of God dwells in believers (1 Cor 3:16; Rom 8:9), so must the word of Messiah reside within the community in

39. Bruce 1957: 282; Dunn 1996: 234; NEB; REB.

40. Calvin 1979a: 216; and similarly Barth and Blanke 1994: 426; Dunn 1996: 236. Cf. Hendriksen (1964: 160) who describes the genitive as "the Christ-word," that is, the revelation which proceeds from and concerns Christ. Lohse (1971: 150) identifies it as the "gospel of Christ" and "word of truth"; O'Brien (1982: 206–7) takes it to mean "the message that centers on Christ, that Word of truth or gospel"; Martin (1973: 115) and Wright (1986: 144) take it as a synonym for Paul's message.

rich abundance and produce its accompanying effects.[41] Importantly, the mechanism by which this word of Messiah is communicated is through instruction (**teaching and admonishing each other**) and in worship (**singing psalms, hymns, and spiritual songs**),[42] and all of this is to occur in the context of **thanksgiving**.[43] If we regard the impartation of the word of Messiah as the goal of teaching, admonishing, and singing, then we are led to the conclusion that teaching is meant to take on a worshipful character while musical praise is to take on a didactic role in order to comprehensively impart the word. Christian teaching is not meant to be dry, but soaked in thankful praise. Similarly, singing is not purposed to be doctrinally benign but should comprise a pointer to the truth of Jesus Christ. In the background to all of this is the notion that whatever Christians do in worship, teaching, work, leisure, or life, they do **in the name of the Lord Jesus, giving thanks to God the Father through him**. That is indicative of the binitarian nature of early Christian worship in making the Father and Son the objects of religious devotion. Jesus, the true image of God, who reconciled the believers to God, remains the fountain from which all thanksgiving overflows and is the one in whom all worship of the Father takes place. What is given to Jesus becomes the Father's, and what is given to the Father is Jesus's since he is the fullness of God (Col 1:19–20; 2:9–10). A fitting summary is given by Theodoret of Cyr: "It is because the Colossians were being directed to worship angels that Paul felt compelled to teach what we read here. This is that they should adorn their words and deeds with the remembrance of Christ the

---

41. Lohse 1971: 150.

42. The differences between these three terms is hard to identify. A psalm (cf. 1 Cor 14:26) may refer to a biblical psalm sung accapella, a hymn (cf. Acts 16:25; Heb 2:12) might include the accompaniment of a musical instrument, and spiritual songs (cf. Rev 5:9; 14:3; 15:3) could include more extemporaneous or even ecstatic forms of melodic praise. See further Lohse 1971: 151. Writing this commentary in the Highlands of Scotland, where a number of denominations mandate the exclusive use of unaccompanied psalmody in worship, makes me want to translate this verse as "psalms, unmusical psalms, and even more psalms" for the amusing edification of my Free Church friends.

43. There is no "and" or grammatical break between the participles **teaching and admonishing** and the nouns that follow, **psalms, hymns, and spiritual songs**. Thus, it seems better to posit the phrasing as a coordinating series that connects the activities of teaching and worship (against the NIV, RSV, NRSV, and agreeing with the NASB, NET, and ESV). See also Lightfoot 1879: 224; Bruce 1957: 283–84; O'Brien 1982: 208–9. On the whole the participles also seem to have an imperatival force (BDF § 468:2).

Lord, that is, they should offer to God the Father the activity of grace through Christ, not through angels."[44]

Fusing the Horizons: Doctrine and Life

Paul has complimented the Colossians on their growth in so far as that he has heard of their love for all the saints (1:4). What he calls them now to do is to reflect that love in action, in behavior, and in attitudes that appropriately reflect a life worthy of the Lord (1:10). In that sense, he prosecutes the integration of doctrine and life and weaves them together throughout this section. The two are inseparable for Paul as an out working of the gospel. Adolf Schlatter pointed out that for Paul the *Denkakt* (thought-act) and the *Lebensakt* (life-act) cannot be divorced from each other. For Paul, one's thought life and practical life are necessarily intertwined.[45] There is no room to accommodate a dry cerebral faith that does not issue forth in action, and there is no place for a Christian lifestyle that is not at once rooted in theological reflection of the gospel. As the Danish philosopher Søren Kierkegaard once said, "As you have lived so have you believed." What ultimately expresses one's true beliefs is not words or statements, but actions (see Jas 2:1–26; 1 John 3:18). Paul does not issue a call for the Colossians to apply his moral philosophy with more stringent rigor or to cultivate the noble virtues as ends in and of themselves. Paul wants the churches of the Lycus Valley to reflect and conform to the power of the new age that is now at work in them through Jesus Christ. Paul wants them to understand themselves as being in-Messiah and to live and love accordingly. We might say that Paul pleads with them not to play CDs on the turntable of a record player since new technology should not be played on old and outdated equipment. That attitude is exemplified in the call to put certain behaviors to death. Biologist E. O. Wilson noticed that colonies of ants communicated through a complex system of chemical pheromones that can indicate certain states such as danger, hunger, mating, and even death. Ants that emitted the pheromone of death were carried away from the nest. Wilson decided to experiment and see what would happen if a fully functional ant was sprayed with the death pheromone. He found that the death-smelling ant,

44. Gorday 2000: 49–50.
45. Schlatter 1909: 7–82.

despite being alive and healthy, was picked up by other ants like a dead ant and carried away from the nest and dumped. The ant would return to the nest and resume work only to have the same process repeated again and again. This provides a fine analogy for Christians who live between the ages and have a life that is hid with Messiah in God but also wait to be revealed with Messiah in glory (Col 3:3–4). They are to put death earthly things even if they are not quite dead yet. What is more, the goal for these ethical precepts is not to improve the individual's respective standing before God, but to contribute to the state of the community as one that abounds in thanksgiving and exudes love. The distinctions that divide, whether ethnic or economic, have no place in the spiritual quickening that accompanies faith in Messiah. Thus, the constitutive aspect for ethics in the new covenant community is new creation in-Messiah.

CHRISTIAN HOUSES IN PAGAN CITIES (3:18—4:1)

[18] Wives, submit to your husbands as is fitting in the Lord. [19] Husbands, love your wives, and do not be harsh with them. [20] Children, obey your parents in every respect, for this is pleasing in the Lord. [21] Fathers, do not antagonize your children, lest they become disheartened. [22] Slaves, obey in every respect those who are your earthly masters, not only when they are watching, as people-pleasers, but with sincerity of heart, fearing the Lord. [23] Whatever you do, work heartily, as to the Lord and not for men, [24] knowing that from the Lord you will receive the reward of inheritance. It is the Lord Messiah you are serving. [25] For the wrongdoer will receive back for the wrong he has done, and there is no partiality. [1] Masters, treat your slaves justly and fairly, knowing that you also have a Lord-Master in heaven.

After the ethical admonitions of 3:1–17, Paul provides some further teaching in 3:18—4:1 about Christian households. This section does not seem to be linked to the teaching of the "philosophy" but comprises a general piece of exhortation about how to live as Christians in a pagan majority environment.[1] We do not know for certain how many Christian households there were in Colossae or the Lycus Valley. We know of at least two house churches in Colossae, operating under the benefaction of Philemon and his wife Apphia (Phlm 1–2), and another in Laodicea under the benefaction (and leadership?) of Nympha (Col 4:15; cf. other

---

1. Cf. in contrast MacDonald (2008: 160, 167), who sees the household code as opposed to the false teaching by reinforcing the Colossians' identity as a spiritual body of believers.

women household heads such as Chloe in 1 Cor 1:11 and Phoebe in Rom 16:1–2). These instructions are addressed to them.

A "household" was more than a domestic dwelling but included the *pater familias* or "head of the house," his wife, children, extended family, slaves, employees, retainers, and often other clientele like political supporters. The Christian household codes (*Haustafeln*) represent teaching addressed to the various members of a household (see Eph 5.:22–33; 1 Pet 2:18—3:7; cf. 1 Tim 2:1–15; 5:1–2; 6:1–2, 17–19; Titus 2:1—3:8; *Did.* 4:9–11; *Barn.* 19:5–7; 1 *Clem.* 1:3—2:1; 21:3–9). They are typified by listing members in binary pairs of husbands/wives, parents/children, and masters/slaves and then defining the mutual relations between the pairs usually in terms of obedience and submission. These codes are most likely derived from Aristotlean or Stoic ethical precepts for the governance of relationships within a household, which were subsequently appropriated by Hellenistic Jewish authors (e.g., Aristotle *Politics* 1.5; Dionysius of Halicarnassus *Ant. rom.* 2.24–27; Seneca *Ep.* 94.1; and in Hellenistic Judaism, e.g., Philo *Hypoth.* 7.1–9; *Decal.* 165–67; Josephus *Ag. Ap.* 2.190–219; Ps.-Phocylides 175–227). A key difference is that whereas the Stoics drew up their household management lists according to the "law of nature," Paul's are clearly patterned after the "law of Messiah" (Gal 6:2) and the "new nature" (Col 3:10).[2] Not everyone particularly likes the Christian household codes. Some feminist scholars regard them as patriarchal and oppressive and often posit "histories" as to how the egalitarian religion of Jesus and Paul was supplanted by the hierarchical and androgynous designs of post-Pauline disciples who wrote the household codes as a means of putting women in their place.[3] Schüssler Fiorenza states: "Colossians shows how a so-called 'enthusiastic' realized eschatological perspective can produce an insistence on patriarchal behaviour as well as an acceptance of the established political-social status quo of inequality and exploitation in the name of Jesus Christ."[4] Schweizer regards them as a "paganizing" of Christian ethics, and Barclay stoically comments that, "for better or worse, the code represents a christianization of traditional rulings on household relationships."[5]

2. Cf. Wright 1986: 147.

3. Cf. e.g. Tamez 2007.

4. Schüssler Fiorenza 1983: 254.

5. Schweizer 1982: 217–20; Barclay 1997: 71.

Yet it must be recognized that Christian authors appropriated these well-known household codes probably for apologetic reasons and as a means of ensuring the commendable conduct of Christian homes before outsiders (see Col 4:5; 1 Thess 4:12).[6] The Christian household codes concern how the lordship of Jesus Christ over a community is to be lived out before the pagan world around them. While these codes are undoubtedly patriarchal, they express that patriarchy in light of mutual obligations of honor and love and clearly censure abuses of authority. They were a necessary way of stabilizing a para- or post-Jewish group that was regarded as religiously sectarian, politically subversive, and socially offensive to cultural elites and civic powers. The Colossian household code is not a reaffirmation of the status quo of pagan ethics, nor a mandate for social revolution, rather, it concerns the authority of the Lord over the household of faith and the mutual obligations that follow from the subordination of all authority under the Lord. In a nutshell, it is the application of the principle of 3:17 to all: "And whatever you do, in word or deed, do all things in the name of the Lord Jesus."[7] Now how would Nympha of Laodicea have responded to this unit of text? Following MacDonald, I would say that her own position as household leader was afforded a degree of protection and respectability by this admonition. She would also, I suspect, have viewed such ethical teaching as obvious and prudent for the world of emerging Christianity.[8]

HOUSEHOLD RELATIONS AMONG HUSBANDS, WIVES, AND CHILDREN (3:18–21)

Paul begins his exhortation about household relations with **Wives, submit to your husbands as is fitting in the Lord**. Wives are to willingly subject themselves to the authority of their husbands as such behavior is appropriate for a women living in the sphere of the Lord's authority. But what actually makes such behavior **fitting** (*anēkō*) is a good question. Is it because it corresponds to the ordering of creation, with male first and woman born second (1 Tim 2:11–15); because of an analogy to Christ/male headship over the church/wives (1 Cor 11:3, 7–9; Eph 5:23–24); or

6. Balch 1981 and others, e.g., Keener 1992: 184–86; Dunn 1996: 251; Lincoln 2000: 653; Balla 2003: 176; MacDonald 2008: 161–62.

7. McL. Wilson 2005: 289.

8. MacDonald 2005: 115.

because it conforms to perceived cultural norms of appropriate marital relations?[9] We are left to guess. The obverse charge to the **Husbands** is to **love your wives** and **do not be harsh with them**. Love is the most supreme ingredient in Christian ethics for Paul (see 3:14).[10] What love in action means is best spelled out by reference to the parallel passage in Ephesians where husbands are commanded to "love your wives as Messiah loved the church and gave himself up for her" (Eph 5:25). In addition, a further admonition upon husbands is to **not be harsh with her**, which is a clear command against brutish and abusive behavior towards wives.

The topic shifts from husbands/wives to parents/children. The children of the household are to **obey your parents in every respect**, and this pertains to all matters since parents, especially fathers and guardians, had legal rights over their children. The justification for this attitude is that it is **pleasing in the Lord**, which is a key motivation for the Christian life according to Paul (Rom 12:1–2; 14:18; 2 Cor 5:9; Eph 5:10; Phil 4:18; see esp. Col 1:10), and honoring one's parents is commanded in the Decalogue (Exod 20:12; Deut 5:16; cf. Matt 15:4–5; 19:19). The command applied to fathers, **do not antagonize your children, lest they become disheartened**, mirrors the relation of husbands/wives where the call for submission is matched by a subsequent command for husbandly authority not to be abused. In regards to children, this means the specific avoidance of behavior that rouses anger and demoralizes rather than builds up.

Household Relations between Masters and Slaves (3:22—4:1)

The slave/master relationship is addressed next in the Colossians household code. Among the Colossian Christians relations between slaves and masters had not always been amicable as the relationship between Philemon and Onesimus shows. Paul affirms not the institution of slavery, which is simply assumed, but how it was to be lived out in Christian community (see "Paul and Slavery" in the introduction). The instructions here must be seen in light of 3:11; the authority of masters over slaves must be situated as part of a wider christological reality of unity in Christ. Unlike 1 Pet 2:18–25, the issue here is not about Christian slaves

9. Cf. Keener 1992: 139–83.
10. Cf. Bird 2008a: 146–48.

owned by non-Christians, but more probably Christian slaves (Christian sometimes by virtue of group conversion, e.g., Acts 11:14; 16:15, 31, 34; 18:8) within Christian households.[11] Paul calls on slaves to obey in all matters their earthly masters and he makes the point with a number of qualifications. First, they are to serve not only **when they are watching, as people-pleasers, but with sincerity of heart, fearing the Lord**. The service rendered is not to be like that of a person constantly checking to see if their master is around so effort and work can be feigned at appropriate moments. Instead, it is to be genuine and sincere service. The accompanying attitude of **fearing the Lord** (see the LXX: Exod 1:17, 21; Lev 19:32; 25:17; Ps 54:20; and NT: 1 Pet 2:17; Rev 11:18; 14:7; 19:5) means reverent submission and obedience to his will. Fear of the Lord is also a mark of loving service to God (Deut 10:12–13) and a sign of God-centered wisdom (Ps 111:10; 112:1; Prov 1:7; 9:10; 15:33; Sir 1:14–27; 19:20; 21:11). Second, they are to **work heartily, as to the Lord and not for men**. The phrase **work heartily** is literally "from the soul" (*ek psuchē*), or from the inner most fabric of one's being. Slaves are not to work only when cornered like a rat in a trap, but without need of supervision and in a genuine spirit of obedience. What is done for earthly masters is really performed for the benefit of the **Lord Messiah** who is the ultimate object of their service. Further justification for such behavior is supplied by Paul in highlighting elements of reward and judgment. Slaves are to conduct themselves as such since they know that **from the Lord you will receive the reward of inheritance**. Slaves had no rights of inheritance unless their masters set them free, but for those who were born in slavery, lived in slavery, and would probably die in slavery, this promise of inheritance was good news. Their lack of honor and inherited possessions would be supplied by the Lord himself as their reward for service to him. But rewards are a two way street. As good behavior is rewarded with an inheritance, so also the **wrongdoer** receives back appropriate punishment for his aberrant ways. That is a principle rooted in the impartiality of God.

Then, as Paul does elsewhere, he again turns the focus from the submissive partner to the master: **Masters, treat your slaves justly and fairly, knowing that you also have a master in heaven**. The masters are themselves slaves to the Lord in heaven and their service to him must be equally appropriate as that of slaves entrusted to their care and service.

11. Cf. Best 1998: 524; Balla 2003: 174.

Whereas Roman law recognized the inalienable legal right of the master over the slave, no such mandate exists in the Christian home, where it is not the rule of Roman law but the impartiality of God that is the final principle for determining what is good and what is wrong. As such, masters are to act in a just and fair manner towards slaves, or else they too risk the threat of punitive justice should they fail to appropriately manage their houses in a righteous way. For instance, whereas slaves were vulnerable to sexual exploitation and abuse by their masters, such activity is inappropriate in light of what Paul says in the Colossian vice lists related to sexual immorality (3:5). This goes to show that there is no mere light coating of Christianity applied to pagan household codes. The relations within the house exist under the auspices of their heavenly Lord, which affects the relational dynamics and ethical imperatives within that household. While we might think of justice for slaves as requiring their emancipation, in Paul's world that was probably unthinkable. But for slaves to hear their masters charged with acting justly towards them and even being threatened with chastisement for unjust behavior, that would have been comforting news. All in all, the Colossian household code is about ordering communal life according to the sovereign authority of the Lord and the wisdom required to live obediently in a pagan environment.

CLOSING WORDS OF EXHORTATION FROM A MISSIONARY FRIEND (4:2–18)

² Continue on in prayer, being watchful in it with thanksgiving; ³ and praying also for us, that God may open a door for us, to declare the word, the mystery of Messiah, because of which I have been bound in prison, ⁴ so that I may reveal it as I am compelled to speak. ⁵ Walk wisely before outsiders, redeeming the time. ⁶ Let your speech always be gracious, seasoned with salt, so that you may know how you ought to answer everyone.

⁷ Tychicus will make known to you all the things concerning me; he is a beloved brother and faithful servant and fellow slave in the Lord. ⁸ I have sent him to you for this purpose, that you may know the things concerning us, and that he might encourage your hearts. ⁹ With him is Onesimus, the faithful and beloved brother, who is one of your own. They will make known to you everything that has transpired here. ¹⁰ Aristarchus my fellow prisoner greets you, and Mark the cousin of Barnabas (concerning whom you received instructions—if he comes to you, receive him), ¹¹ and Jesus who is called Justus. These are the only men from the circumcision among my fellow workers for the kingdom of God, and they have been an encouragement to me. ¹² Epaphras, who is one of your own, a slave of Messiah Jesus, greets you, always struggling for you in prayer, that you may stand mature and fully assured in all of God's will. ¹³ For I testify to him, that he has worked hard for you and for those in Laodicea and in Hierapolis. ¹⁴ Luke the beloved physician and Demas greet you. ¹⁵ Greet the brothers and sisters in Laodicea, and to Nympha and the church in her house. ¹⁶ And after this let-

ter has been read among you, have it read also in the church of the Laodiceans; and see that you also read the letter from Laodicea. [17] And say to Archippus, "See to it that you fulfill the ministry which you have received in the Lord." [18] I, Paul, write this greeting with my own hand. Remember my chains. The grace be with you.

The epistle rounds off with some final exhortations, a commendation of the ministry of Paul and his coworkers, final greetings, and the grace. This section also recaps many of the earlier themes of the letter including that of thanksgiving (1:3, 11; 3:15, 17 and 4:2), gospel proclamation (1:15–29 and 4:3), the mystery of the Messiah (1:26–27; 2:2 and 4:3), and the quality of Epaphras's ministry (1:7 and 4:12–13). Here Paul and his coauthors seek, above all, to cement the relationship between the Colossian believers and the Pauline churches. This is emphasized in a number of ways. To begin with, Paul emphasizes (three times no less) that he wants them to be informed of his own situation, which is why Tychicus and Onesimus have been dispatched for the task of transmitting firsthand accounts of Paul's situation to them (4:7–9). On top of that, there is also mentioned twice a reference to Onesimus and Epaphras as those who are **one of your own** (lit. "from you" in 4:9, 12). In other words, the Colossians already are involved in the Pauline mission via Epaphras and Onesimus, and that solidarity is reinforced by making them fully aware of the state of affairs as they pertain to Paul and his companions. Paul deliberately presumes on their support and interest, which, if they renege on it by subscribing to the philosophy, potentially brings shame upon them. This reaffirmation of a special bond between the Pauline churches and the Colossians means that they have an obligation to respond accordingly as those treated as supporters and benefactors of the Pauline mission. This assumes a set of obligations on their part in terms of continued adherence to shared beliefs and upholding standards of conduct if reciprocal relations are to be maintained. In other words, because they *belong* to the Pauline churches they are indebted to continue *believing* the Pauline gospel. Paul calls on them to live up to the praises that he has heaped upon them in 1:2–8. Paul demonstrates that their role as partners with the Pauline mission and their sense of shared identity with other Christian believers is intimately bound up with the gospel of the mystery of the Messiah. Put this way, their agreement with the gospel is required in order to uphold the honor ascribed to them by Paul and to reinforce the mutual affections between them.

Viewed from this perspective, it is possible to see how the closing section relates to the risk posed by the philosophy. It comes down not just to a matter of "what do you believe?" but "to whom do you belong?" If they believe in the Messiah, then they belong to the Messiah and to the communities (like those associated with Paul) that proclaim him and live obediently before him. The Colossians are treated as benefactors, supporters, and partners in the **kingdom of God**, but they will bring shame on themselves if they do not act accordingly or if they embrace the philosophy with its diminishment of the status of Messiah Jesus. What is more, the reference to the **circumcision** in 4:11 is perhaps an indirect jibe at the teachers and a further indication of the philosophy's links to local synagogues.[1] Paul, though himself a Jew, has had relatively little assistance in his endeavors from Jews not believing in Jesus (see 1 Thess 2:15). Persons such as Jesus called Justus and Timothy are invaluable to Paul's service, but they are the exceptions. Thus the Colossians should not think that allying themselves to the local synagogue will necessarily translate into joint endeavors in kingdom work; the realities from Paul's own experience have proven otherwise.

Prayer, Proclamation, and Walking in Wisdom (4:2–6)

After establishing the nature of relations in Christian households (largely to offset allegations that Christians are anti-social radicals), Paul proceeds to exhort the Colossians in the life of faithfulness that he has already spoken of (1:4; 2:5). They are to **continue on in prayer**, in the sense of persistent dedication to the discipline of its practice (see Acts 1:14; 6:4; Rom 12:12). The verb *proskartereō* is an imperative and plural; it is a corporate command to the entire Colossian community to be devoted to prayer. Communal prayer is a means of **being watchful** by ensuring vigilant readiness in times of grave danger, and it means keeping one's spiritual eyes open. Prayer is also to be offered with **thanksgiving**, which Paul himself models in Colossians (1:3–14) and Philemon (4–5). Even

---

1. Cf. Wall 1993: 172; Dunn 1996: 278.

though Colossians has much to say in response to a perceived doctrinal threat, the letter is hardly doctrinaire and its content is permeated with calls for thanksgiving, praise, prayer, and conduct befitting God's holy people. Paul specifically asks that prayer be offered for him and his coworkers, that **God may open a door for us, to declare the word, the mystery of Messiah** (on "doors" for mission work see 1 Cor 16:9; 2 Cor 2:12; Acts 14:27). Ephesians 6:19–20 says much the same but refers only to Paul, with "me/I" instead of "us." This is a prayer for God's initiative, assistance, and direction in opening up avenues for them to continue their evangelistic task, described in 1:28 as proclaiming, admonishing, and teaching all persons. Incarceration, it seems, happened to Paul as a result of his missionary work, but that itself was no absolute hindrance to Paul's evangelistic activities. In fact, his imprisonment may have even spurned others on in their own respective tasks (see Phil 1:12–14). Yet Paul still covets their prayerful intercession for the sake of his mission. Paul and his colleagues want to **declare the word**, and in Colossians this "word" is an announcement ultimately coming from God and about the Messiah (1:5, 25; 3:16). The language of proclamation clearly takes on an apocalyptic character as Paul hopes to **reveal** the message, and the same word (*phaneroō*) is used about the eschatological manifestation of the Messiah at his *parousia* in 3:4. Similarly the **mystery of the Messiah** (1:26–27; 2:2–3) relates to the curtain of the heavenly mystery being drawn back to give a fuller view of a reality that, though unseen to the eye, touches heaven and earth and ultimately impacts the entire course of cosmic existence through the exalted Messiah. It is the secret plan of God to bring salvation to the whole world in, by, and through the Lord Jesus Christ. Hence, the announcement of the gospel is an apocalyptic event that includes a summons to its audience for faith and obedience towards the world's true Lord (1:15–20), an offer of reconciliation (1:20, 22) and forgiveness (1:14; 2:13), a warning of judgment (1:28; 3:6, 25), a declaration of God's triumph over evil through the cross (2:15), and a gift of hope to a world that was brutal, cold, and dark (1:12–14, 23). It is no wonder that Paul felt **compelled to speak** out of great conviction, genuine pathos, and with deep concern for others (see 1 Cor 9:22; 10:33; Rom 9:1–5). This compulsion came out of a belief that God's plan to rescue the world is being wrought through him, with God determining both the ends and the means of his glory (see 1:29).

Paul turns to the community's responsibility to further this mission in their own midst. Notably, he does not call upon them to emulate strictly in a local context the task that he has to herald the gospel. Not everyone is called to be an apostle or evangelist. They are to be wise in the world, gracious in speech, and ready to answer about their faith. First, at several points Paul has something to say about their **walk** before the Lord (1:10; 2:6) and here it is a matter of their daily life before outsiders. Christianity is not a private religion lived in the interiorized safety of the mind, but is lived in partnership with other believers in the public sphere. We have already seen that the household code in 3:18—4:1 is probably given to help the Colossian households order themselves so as to avoid accusation that they are anti-social radicals. That was something that was quite possible given the situation in First Corinthians where excessive spiritual enthusiasm seems to have overpowered all sense of order, as well as in Gnostic exegesis of Gal 3:28/Col 3:11, which took Paul's remarks in a radical direction and eradicated all social and gender distinctions through a hyper-Platonic anthropology. To walk **wisely** requires giving no reason for insult, doing good to win the favor of others, and living in such a way as to attract praise and positive curiosity (similarly, see e.g., 1 Cor 10:32–33; Phil 2:14–16). This is **redeeming the time** or making the most of their opportunities in the situation that they are in for the gospel. Obedience is not an end in itself, but is for the benefit of **outsiders**, those that have not received the word of the Messiah.[2] Second, Paul adds **let your speech always be gracious, seasoned with salt**, which builds on both Jewish and Hellenistic wisdom traditions about the use of speech. Similar statements can be found elsewhere in the New Testament, especially in Eph 4:29 and 5:4 about avoiding vulgar conversation and in Jas 3:2–12 concerning use and abuse of the tongue. A godly walk must be accompanied by godly talk. Third, this instruction is given **so that you may know how you ought to answer every one** and this presupposes a willingness and opportunity to expound one's faith and beliefs before others (see 1 Pet 3:15–16). A wise and God-centered pattern of life with characteristic speech pervaded with graciousness provides the means by which they find opportunities to answer outsiders who ask genuine questions about their faith. Whereas Paul is very much involved in active proclamation, he envisages the Colossians exhibiting an attractive pres-

2. Barth and Blanke 1994: 454–55.

ence towards outsiders with a view to inviting them to share in the faith and community of the Lord. These instructions are for a church expected to hold their own in the market places, baths, forums, and meal tables of the city and to win attention by the attractiveness of their way of life and their manner of speech.[3]

FINAL INSTRUCTION AND GREETING (4:7–18)

News of Paul's situation is to be conveyed by **Tychicus** and **Onesimus** who are the couriers of the letter to the Colossians. The former is named elsewhere in the New Testament as a believer from Asia, perhaps Ephesus, and he seems to have been a favorite envoy of Paul (Acts 20:4; Eph 6:21; 2 Tim 4:12; Titus 3:12). **Onesimus** was the formerly estranged slave of Philemon with whom he had been reconciled and by whom he was returned to Paul as requested by Paul (Phlm 13). Both men are described as **beloved brothers** and as **faithful** (Tychicus is also described as a **servant** and **fellow slave**), which echoes Paul's description of the Colossians themselves in 1:2. The news that they pass on is intended to **encourage your hearts**, which may be a veiled way of saying that they will exhort the Colossians to remain true to the gospel in light of the intrusive philosophy.[4]

Paul proceeds to name three Jewish Christian coworkers with him who also send their greetings. The first is **Aristarchus**, who is described as a **fellow prisoner** and is to be identified with Aristarchus from Acts, a Macedonian from Thessalonica (Acts 19:29; 20:4; 27:2; Phlm 24). The second is John **Mark**, the Cypriot Jewish Christian who at one time deserted Paul (Acts 13:13; 15:37–41) but seems to have been reconciled to him at some point prior to this (Phlm 24; 2 Tim 4:11). In a later time, Mark was part of Peter's circle in Rome (1 Pet 5:13). The Colossians have already received **instructions** about a possible visit by John Mark (from a previous letter or an oral report) and Paul underscores that he may send John Mark to them in the future and they should **receive him** accordingly. The final coworker Paul mentions, **Jesus who is called Justus**, is a Jewish Christian who added a "t" to his name for a transition from *Iēsous*

---

3. Dunn 1996: 267.
4. Cf. O'Brien 1982: 248.

to *Ioustos.*[5] These three are described as coming from the **circumcision**, which is most probably a designation for a Jew (Gal 2:8–9; Phil 3:3; Titus 1:10). These are the only Jewish Christians among Paul's **fellow workers** and this remark might have a slight barb on the end of it to warn against excessive fraternizing with local synagogues in Colossae. Christians in Asia did not always receive the best response from Jewish communities as evident from the riot over Paul in Ephesus (Acts 19:33–34) and the scolding remarks in Revelation where Jews of Smyrna and Philadelphia are called "a synagogue of Satan" (Rev 2:9; 3:9).

Their common work relates to the **kingdom of God**, which, despite the paucity of its references in Paul's letters compared to the Gospels, is no less important. It has four primary spheres of meaning: (1) the power of God which has invaded the present time through a display of powerful deeds (1 Cor 4:20); (2) a term reflecting the totality of the "now" experience of God's salvific blessings (Rom 14:17; Col 1:13; cf. Acts 19:8; 20:25; 28:23, 31); (3) a future state that believers have been called into and can expect to enter into unless they disqualify themselves with incessant immoral behavior (1 Cor 6:9–10; 15:50; Gal 5:21; Eph 5:5; 1 Thess 2:12; 2 Thess 1:5; 2 Tim 4:1; cf. Acts 14:22); and (4) the manifestation of God's reign on earth at the *parousia* of Jesus the Messiah (1 Cor 15:24, 50–57; 2 Tim 4:1, 18). The usage of kingdom here in 4:11 is clearly in line with 1:13 where "kingdom" stands for the salvation of God revealed in the saving reign of the Son.

A final trio of coworkers is then mentioned as sending greetings. First, **Epaphras**, whose qualities are lauded by Paul very much as a continuation from 1:7 where he was called a "beloved fellow slave" and "a faithful servant of the Messiah." Epaphras was probably the "evangelist" and founding "pastor" of the churches of the Lycus Valley and now operates in Paul's own immediate circle. He is called again a **slave of Messiah Jesus**, which highlights the devoted nature of his service. Epaphras is described as **struggling for you in prayer**, which not only highlights his pastoral concern for the Colossians, but shows that he fulfills the exhortation about devotion in prayer in 4:2. The purpose of his prayer is that they **stand mature** and be **fully assured in all of God's will**, and this prayer reflects the same goals that Paul has for his ministry in 1:28 and 2:2 about

---

5. Note the other figures with this name in Acts: Joseph called Barsabbas, "who was know as Justus" (Acts 1:23), and "Titius Justus," who was a God-fearer in Corinth (Acts 18:7).

bringing believers to maturity and full assurance. Such traits describe persons who are well developed, confident in themselves and in God, and not easily given over to unwholesome influence (see Eph 4:14: "We must no longer be children, tossed to and fro and blown about by every wind of doctrine, by people's trickery, by their craftiness in deceitful scheming" [NRSV]). Epaphras's prayer is that they have the maturity, wisdom, and confidence to resist the incursions of the teachers with their philosophy. Paul testifies that Epaphras has **worked hard** for them and for the other churches of the Lycus Valley (Laodicea and Hierapolis), therefore, they should take pride in his efforts as their representative and honor him by holding to the pattern of teaching that he passed on to them. Greetings are also extended from **Luke the beloved physician**[6] and **Demas** who were prominent members in the Pauline circle (Phlm 24; 2 Tim 4:10–11).

Paul requests that greetings also be extended to the **brothers and sisters in Laodicea, and to Nympha and the church in her house**, which is probably the other major household church in the Lycus Valley. If someone was travelling to Colossae from Ephesus they would naturally go through Laodicea on the way. A **letter** had already been delivered to those in Laodicea and both households are to exchange letters and to read them for the exhortation of the believers. The congregational reading of the letter highlights the oral and aural nature of early Christian texts. Reading was not so much a matter of private study, but a communal act undertaken in the context of worship or shared meals. But what was this letter to the Laodiceans? It might be Ephesians, which we have grounds to suspect was a circular letter for the Pauline churches of Asia given that "in Ephesus" in Eph 1:1 does not occur in some manuscripts (P[46] $\aleph$* B* 424[c] 1739).[7] What is more, both letters refer to the arrival of Tychicus, which is probably no small coincidence (Eph 6:21; Col 4:7). Marcion purportedly designated the epistle as "to the Laodiceans," which, though tertiary evidence at best is still illuminating. The fact is that we simply do not know for sure what the letter was, but Ephesians is probably the best guess that we can make.[8]

---

6. This is the only place where Luke's vocation is made known to us, and, given that he is not mentioned as among those of the "circumcision," probably means that he was a Gentile.

7. Cf. Lightfoot 1879: 272–98.

8. The proposal of John Knox (1959) that the letter to the Laodiceans is in fact Philemon has, despite its intriguing qualities, not met with wide approval. There are five

The penultimate exhortation pertains to **Archippus** who appears to have been a leader of some group possibly linked to the house of Philemon (see Phlm 2, where he is called a "fellow soldier"). The remark is not addressed to him personally, instead it is given to the Colossians in general: **Say to Archippus, "See to it that you fulfil the ministry which you have received in the Lord."** Notably, the word for **Say** is in the plural and the believers are corporately to encourage Archippus to fulfill his ministry as something exercised in the sphere of the Lord's authority. What that ministry exactly was, is not stated. It could be to preach, teach, or relate to the collection for the Jerusalem church. What I find plausible is the suggestion that it refers to Archippus taking Epaphras's place, but that is admittedly conjectural.[9] Whatever his "service" was, Archippus is either struggling or in need of encouragement. If he remains one of the few "pastoral" leaders in the churches, his lot might not be a pleasant one in having to contend with the aftermath of the Philemon/Onesimus incident, coping with the absence of Epaphras, dealing with the philosophy when still himself a "young" believer, and now facing the presence of Tychicus and Onesimus (and perhaps even John Mark still to come) who may usurp or upstage his own status and position within the churches in the Lycus Valley. One must wonder if behind these statements there lies an element of "pastoral politics," as Archippus has not handled the situation in Colossae well, resulting in Paul and his coworkers feeling the need to write them a letter exhorting them quite forcefully on certain matters, reminding them of Epaphras's legacy, and parachuting in a cohort of Pauline coworkers to do any necessary triage in the Lycus Valley. Then again, perhaps Archippus himself called for assistance. Either way this last statement is an affirmation of Archippus's service and a recognition of his place in the leadership of the Colossian church.

---

planks in his argument: (1) Archippus was a deacon in Colossae, while Philemon lived in Laodicea; (2) it was Archippus rather than Philemon who was the slave owner of Onesimus; (3) the letter to the Laodiceans is this letter to Philemon; (4) the purpose of the letter to Philemon is to force Archippus, through Philemon's personal influence, to release Onesimus so that he might in the future work with Paul; and (5) Onesimus was finally manumitted and eventually became bishop of Ephesus. See criticisms of Knox's argument in Fitzmyer 2000: 14–17.

9. Calvin 1979a: 231; Gnilka 1980: 246; Fitzmyer 2000: 88 (citing Caird and Lohmeyer). In *Apostolic Constitutions* 7.46 Archippus is mentioned as a one time bishop of Laodicea, Jerome thinks him bishop of Colossae, Chrysostom has him as one of the clergy, and Pelagius thinks him a deacon (Gorday 2000: 311).

Finally, the letter closes with Paul's autograph. He urges them to remember his **chains** as a vivid image of the physical nature of his imprisonment. The chains are themselves further proof that Paul really is a "servant" of the gospel (1:23, 25) and is "filling up what is lacking in the afflictions of the Messiah" (1:24). The apostle then closes with the benediction **the grace be with you,** a fitting close to a letter that commends the "grace of God in all its truth" (1:6).

Fusing the Horizons: Christian Leaders

In light of Col 4:2–17, how is the pastor, elder, Sunday school teacher, youth worker, and Bible study leader to serve their congregations? Christian leaders can take a lot away from this.

1. *Prayer and Word.* Central to any Christian ministry must be the discipline of prayer and instruction in the Word. This was very much central in the ministry of the apostles in the early Jerusalem church (Acts 6:4), and a similar pattern is found in Col 4:2–3. Ministers of the new covenant are to boldly declare the word of God to those both outside and within the church. They are also to "struggle" in prayer for others. How many Sunday School teachers, hospital chaplains, pastors, Christian professors, or leaders in campus ministries can honestly say that they struggle in prayer for those entrusted to their instruction and spiritual care? One of my seminary professors told me a story about how he was at an all-day conference for Christian ministers from various denominations in a small country town. Every couple of hours the local priest, who was hosting the event, would rise from the table, ring a large bell in the church tower and return to the meeting about ten minutes later. When asked why he did that (especially as it was so annoying and disruptive for the meeting) he replied that every few hours during the day he would pray for at least ten minutes for the people in the local township, and ringing the bell was how he let them know that their priest was now praying for them. We do not have to ring bells or bang gongs, but we need to let the flock under our care know that we are faithfully praying for them. They will be genuinely consoled and encouraged to know that their youth pastor, Christian friend, chaplain, professor, deacon, or parish priest is wrestling for them with prayers and petitions before the throne of God.

2. *Servant and Slave.* Common in Colossians is the description of Paul's coworkers as "fellow servants" and "fellow slaves." One has to ask whether views of ministry in affluent Western cultures have been adversely influenced by corporate styles of leadership and images of success. If one is going into the "ministry" it should mean that one is going to become a servant of God, or more specifically, one is going to become a servant of God by serving the people of God.[10] But somewhere along the line we began to think of ourselves as "religious professionals" rather than "ministers." In fact, some churches have even reorganized their leadership structures to reflect corporate models, with the senior pastor becoming a *de facto* CEO and other staff becoming vice presidents of marketing, recruitment, human resources, youth services, and estates. The language of the New Testament is not that of "reverend" or "senior pastor" but of "slaves" and "servants" of Jesus the Christ. What we want ourselves to be called obviously reflects how we want ourselves to be perceived by others. Are we religious professionals on par with corporate professionals? Or are we ministers of the new covenant, called to service not greatness, full of humility not boasting, inspired by heaven not earthly recognition, and filling our flesh with afflictions not filling our pockets with cash? Servants and slaves seek not honor for themselves, but honor and glory for their master.

3. *The Archippus Factor.* I have been involved in a variety of Christian ministries in the military, in public schools, in homes, in churches, and on university campuses. I have never been a pastor myself; nonetheless, I have much experience in training them for ministry in the Word of God and teaching them how to think theologically. One thing I have learned is that all ministry, especially pastoral ministry, can be tiring, difficult, discouraging, draining, and often thankless work. Pastors often see the worst side of Christians, they can find themselves hounded by people with constant needs, counseling people with marital problems, having to mediate between disputing persons, and working hard to prepare sermons that are not always appreciated let alone heeded. All ministers, like Archippus, are in desperate need of regular encouragement, reassurance, and gratitude. They need to be told, by the church and by individuals, to "fulfill your ministry which you received in the Lord." Under times of upheaval and adversity this is all the more important. I was once in a church in North Queensland, Australia where the pastor was preaching a two part series on "The Bible and Homosexuality." After the first sermon the

---

10. I would add that the *diakoneō/diakonos* word group for "serving" and "servant/deacon" indicates activity rather than status (see Hentschel 2007).

local gay rights group heard about the sermon series, said some slanderous things about him in a newspaper interview (i.e., accusing him of saying that AIDS is God's punishment against homosexuals, which he never said) and planned to stage a protest at the church the next Sunday. There was a mid-week prayer meeting planned, and we learned that all four major TV stations were sending crews to film the event. The pastor looked visibly tired and worn out by the stress and tension (we were all taken by surprise over how quickly and intensely the whole affair erupted), but at that midweek meeting there were no calls for him to back down, no criticism of his leadership, no hate mongering against homosexuals, but prayer and encouragement for the pastor to finish what he started and to boldly proclaim the word of God. It was a word of encouragement that he desperately needed. The new covenant community needs to be one where encouragement for its slaves and servants is not a rarity but a regular event, especially in times of trial and hardship. This is the Archippus Factor!

PHILEMON

LETTER OPENING, GREETING, AND THANKSGIVING (1–7)

Paul, a prisoner for Messiah Jesus, and Timothy our brother. To Philemon our beloved fellow worker [2] and Apphia our sister and Archippus our fellow soldier, and to the church in your house. [3] Grace to you and peace from God our Father and the Lord Jesus *Christ*. [4] I thank my God always when I remember you in my prayers, [5] hearing of your love and faithfulness which you have toward the Lord Jesus and to all the saints, [6] in order that the sharing of your faith may become effective in the full knowledge of every good thing that is in us for the sake of Messiah. [7] For I have taken much joy and comfort from your love, because the hearts of the saints have been refreshed through you brother.

The letter to Philemon is a mere 335 words, yet it raises crucial issues about slavery and the ethics of pastoral persuasion. It is the final letter in the Pauline corpus and among the most personal and pastoral in the New Testament canon. The letter is addressed primarily to Philemon but also includes Apphia, Archippus, and the church in his house. This means that we have a private letter that is placed into a wider congregational setting as the context in which the drama of Onesimus's flight and the effectiveness of Paul's mediation is played out. A household matter is put before a household church. Moreover, it is a letter that draws us into the narrative and social world of the apostle and the associated challenges that Paul faced as a missionary pastor.[1] Notably, in the letter opening, Paul offers thanksgiving praises to Philemon for the very virtues that he hopes he will express in resolving the matter concerning Onesimus.

1. Cf. Petersen 1985.

133

The opening self-identification of **Paul** is uniquely spelled out as a **prisoner for Messiah Jesus,** which is no doubt literal (see Phlm 9; Eph 3:1) and refers to an imprisonment most probably during his time in Ephesus. Perhaps the designation attempts to evoke a deliberate pathos, since the legal position of a slave was not dissimilar to that of a prisoner and so adds further relevance to the exhortation that Paul will make for a slave. Paul is not a prisoner of "Caesar" or the "state" but of the **Messiah Jesus,** since it is the cause of the Messiah and the gospel for which he is in chains. As elsewhere, **Timothy** is included as cosender (1 Thess 1:1; Phil 1:1; Col 1:1–2; 2 Thess 1:1), but his involvement in the composition of the letter, unlike Colossians, is probably indirect. Paul writes this short and very personal letter with his own hand (v. 19). The addressee is **Philemon,** which was a fairly popular name in Phrygia, common in inscriptions and papyri.[2] He is described as a **beloved fellow worker,** which associates him with the Pauline mission, though in what sense is undefined (in later church tradition he is identified as the bishop of Colossae).[3] Philemon may have some role in the leadership of the church that meets in his house, along with Archippus, or else he has contributed to Paul's missionary endeavors at some point in the past. The latter is more likely in view of the reference to "partnership" in v. 17, which suggests a sharing of resources. Also named is **Apphia,** who is probably Philemon's wife or sister. This again is a common Phrygian name, and in one instance it is found on a tombstone in the ruins of Colossae: "Hermas to his wife Apphia, the daughter of Trypho."[4] Regardless of her actual relation to Philemon, as the lady of the house she would have been the primary overseer of slaves in the dwelling and in the daily operation of the household. She may also have held some formal office in the house church that met in her house. **Archippus** is named next. He probably was the primary fill-in pastor in Colossae given Epaphras's absence. Archippus was called to discharge some kind of "ministry" in the interim while Epaphras was away (Col 4:17). Importantly, the letter is also addressed, even if obliquely, to the **church in your house.** The **your** is ambiguous as it could refer to a house belonging to either Philemon, Apphia, or Archippus, but the former seems more probable given that Philemon is the first named addressee

2. *NDIEC* 3:91; 5:144.

3. *Apostolic Constitutions* 7.46.

4. Cited from Barth and Blanke 2000: 254.

and as an owner of slaves he would most likely have a dwelling capable of hosting several persons. Christians met in a variety of places and settings (outdoors, rented rooms, shops, etc.). House churches were common if a congregational member had a suitable space available for use in prayer, Scripture reading, and shared meals. The church that meets in Philemon's house remains on the periphery of the letter as Philemon's response to Paul is to be played out before them. Paul deliberately draws in the congregation as a whole in order to make them stakeholders in the outcome of his request.

Paul includes his customary grace and prayerful thanksgiving for Philemon. Special themes here are faith(fulness), the saints, joy, comfort, and refreshment, which will all appear again in the letter. The reason for Paul's thanksgiving is Philemon's **love and faithfulness** for the **Lord Jesus and to all the saints**. Indeed, Paul intends to appeal to Philemon to love Onesimus as a brother and to obey Paul's request out of gratitude to him. Paul also prays that **the sharing of your faith may become effective in the full knowledge of every good thing that is in us for the sake of Messiah.** This **sharing** refers to an overflow of goodness and kindness, much like a faith-in-action-through-love exhibited towards other believers (see Gal 5:6; 6:6; 1 Thess 5:15; Rom 15:2). Paul prays that other Christians, not least himself, participate in the good expression of Philemon's faith. It is both a prayer of thanks and a plea for continued generosity by Philemon. This sharing becomes **effective** through the fullness of **knowledge**. That knowledge pertains to how the good that Christians do benefits other Christians and thus Christ himself. Charles Moule notes that "good" is ordinarily mentioned by Paul as something that is done or performed rather than the object of knowledge.[5] The **good thing** in question then is the good conduct that accompanies the sharing of one's faith, which springs out of the abundant goodness that one has already received. Put simply, out of the abundance of good things that Philemon has received through the Lord Jesus he is now to display goodness to others. The prepositional phrase **for the sake of Messiah** is ambiguous (lit. "into/for Messiah"; contrast "that we may do for Christ" [NRSV]; "every good thing we have in Christ" [NIV]; "all the good we can do for Christ" [NJB]). The preposition *eis* is probably purposive and suggests that the values embodied by the Messiah are upheld and honored in the benevolence of

---

5. Moule 1957: 143.

Christians towards their brothers and sisters in the faith.[6] In other words, Paul lauds (and will appeal) to an identical benevolence in Philemon. A further reason for Paul's thanksgiving is that Philemon's **love** for the saints occasions Paul's **joy and comfort**. This extends not only to Paul but to other **saints** (i.e., those of Paul's circle who know of Philemon, such as Epaphras) who have been **refreshed** by Philemon. The connotation here is of relief from toil and frustration through assistance. Once more the compliment implies a question. Philemon has been a means of comfort and consolation to others before; on the issue relating to Onesimus, will he be so again?

---

6. Cf. Lohse 1971: 194; and CSB, who opt for "the glory of Christ."

THE PATHOS AND PERSUASION
OF THE APOSTLE (8–22)

8 Therefore, though I am bold enough in Messiah to command you to do what is fitting 9 on account of love I prefer to appeal to you—I, Paul, an old man and now a prisoner of Messiah Jesus—10 I appeal to you concerning my child, Onesimus, whom I gave birth to during imprisonment. 11 (Formerly he was useless to you, but now to you and to me he is useful) 12 I am sending him, who is my very heart, back to you. 13 I wished to keep him with me, in order that he might serve me on your behalf during my imprisonment for the gospel, 14 but I wished to do nothing without your consent in order that your goodness might not be by compulsion but of your own free decision. 15 Perhaps for this reason he was separated from you for a short time, so that you might have him back forever, 16 no longer as a slave but more than a slave, as a beloved brother—especially to me, but how much more to you, both in the flesh and in the Lord. 17 If, then, you have partnership with me, receive him as you would receive me. 18 If he has wronged you, or owes you anything, charge that to me. 19 I, Paul, write this with my own hand: I will repay it—to say nothing of you owing me your very own self. 20 Yes, brother, I want some benefit from you in the Lord. Renew my heart in Messiah. 21 Confident of your obedience, I write to you, knowing that you will do even more than I ask. 22 At the same time, prepare a guest room for me, for I am hoping that through your prayers I will be graciously restored to you.

The body of the letter is contained in vv. 8–22 where Paul makes his plea for Onesimus by acting as an intermediary. Paul describes his own situation as a prisoner and elderly man and recaps his relationship to Onesimus, including Onesimus's conversion, which must now be factored into Philemon's response. There is a deliberate play on Onesimus's name as "useful"; Paul hints at his desire to have Onesimus returned to him as an assistant. The intercession includes Paul's willingness to cover any debts incurred by Onesimus's error and he reminds Philemon of his own indebtedness to Paul. Philemon's debt would be covered with Philemon's obedience to Paul's request.

The transition to the letter body is marked by **therefore**, which seeks to apply Paul's thanksgiving and prayerful activity to the matter at hand. While Paul is **bold enough in Messiah to command** Philemon to respond positively to his request, he is reluctant to do so. Paul was a figure of audacity, bravado, chutzpah, and no holds barred arguing. When combined with his apostolic credentials, Paul might well order Philemon to submit to his authority. Yet what Paul wants is for Philemon to do **what is fitting** or morally appropriate to the concern that he is about to raise. The response should be fitting to Philemon as both a slave owner and as a Christian, which would be the opposite of acting out of spite, anger, or as a grieved slave owner. Paul does not issue a command, but rather prefers to make an **appeal** on the basis of **love**. Paul willingly forfeits the demand of obedience that his apostolic authority could rightly claim and instead appeals to Philemon's sense of goodness and kind affection.

Paul appeals in person as an **old man** and a **prisoner of Messiah Jesus,** which evidently is meant to tug on the heart strings at least a little since it highlights his vulnerability and the cost of the service borne by him. He then gets to the substance of his appeal for **my child, Onesimus, whom I gave birth to during imprisonment.** Some time during Paul's imprisonment (how and why we don't know for sure) Onesimus came into Paul's company and was converted to faith in Jesus. Paul could often refer to himself as a father to his children (1 Cor 4:14–17) and the maternal language of giving birth to a child is not in anyway foreign to Paul either (Gal 4.19). The image here could be paternal (e.g., "whose father I became" [ESV]; cf. NRSV, NET, NJB),[1] but I prefer a maternal image of "giving birth" because (1) in the New Testament *gennaō* has the most

---

1. Cf. Petersen 1985: 128.

common meaning of a mother giving birth, and (2) Paul refers to his *splanchna* in verses 8 and 10, which, though I have translated as **heart** (the seat of one's emotions), could also be translated as "womb." Thus, as in Gal 4:19, Paul exhibits an intense motherly care for the welfare and well-being of his spiritual progeny.[2] Paul uses positive and affectionate language for Onesimus throughout the epistle, referring to Onesimus as "my child" (v. 10), "my very heart" (v. 12), "beloved brother" (v. 17), and in Colossians as his "beloved and faithful brother' (Col 4:9). The point is to underscore Paul's deep affection for Onesimus. The affection has grown out of Onesimus's conversion and this has wrought a transformation in Onesimus in that he was formerly **useless** but is now **useful**. This is on account of the step of faith that the slave made while seeking Paul's intercession on his behalf. There is a double play on words here. First, the name Onesimus (*Onēsimos*) means "useful, profitable" and was a common slave name in Asia Minor.[3] What is meant by **useless** (*achrēstos*) and **useful** (*euchrēstos*) is unclear; it might be retrospective and comparative, that is, Onesimus was formerly useless to us all, but now he has genuine usefulness (so much so that Paul would like to enlist him into his service). Second, there might also be a deliberate play on the words *achrēstos* and *euchrēstos* since they sound similar to *Christos* ("Christ") or *Christianos* ("Christian"). As such, Onesimus was formerly *achrēstos* when he was without Christ, but he is now *euchrēstos* as a *Christianos*.[4]

Despite the usefulness of Onesimus and Paul's deep affection for him, this itself did not override Paul's sense of obligation to return Onesimus back to his master. In vv. 13–14 the apostle expresses his heavy-hearted willingness to return Onesimus to Philemon as well as stating his desire to keep him. Paul remarks that he would very much have liked to have retained the services of Onesimus for the reason that **he might serve me on your behalf during my imprisonment for the gospel**. The service (*diakoneō*) that Onesimus might conceivably offer could be manifold. Many slaves were literate, well-educated, and capable administrators. Onesimus might provide service as a Pauline messenger (2 Cor 8:19–20; 9:3; Eph 6:22), discharge an unspecified ministry of some kind (Matt 8:15; 27:55; John 12:26; Acts 19:22; 2 Tim 1:18; 1 Pet 4:10–11), or perhaps even

2. See discussion in Barth and Blanke 2000: 329–35.

3. *NDIEC* 4:179–81; Fitzmyer 2000: 107.

4. Cf. Baur 2003 [1873–75]: 478; Winter 1987: 4–5.

occupy the office of deacon (Acts 6:2; Rom 16:1; 1 Tim 3:10, 13; though this is perhaps unlikely for a new convert). Given Onesimus's travels, the first option of acting as Paul's messenger or delegate is probably in mind and Onesimus is groomed to be one of Paul's many emissaries.[5] Paul presumes upon an obligation by Philemon to render service, a service that may be vicariously performed by Onesimus in Philemon's place. This service is not rendered only to Paul but to the cause of the **gospel** for which Paul is imprisoned. Paul goes on to restate the same point, only differently, by referring to his unwillingness to retain Onesimus in his service without Philemon's **consent**. The reason for not presuming upon Philemon's compliance to Paul's request is so that **your goodness might not be by compulsion but of your own free decision**. This **goodness** obviously implies Philemon either giving him a slave for free or, more likely, manumitting Onesimus so that he can serve as a freedman as part of Paul's circle of co-workers. Such goodness would be an obvious example of the "sharing of your faith" as referred to in v. 6.

Paul moves to intercede directly to Philemon for Onesimus and engages the matter of their estrangement. Paul acts here as a "friend of the master" and seeks to achieve a reconciliation that affirms that Onesimus had done wrong but is forgivable. Paul consciously tries to maintain Philemon's honor and reputation in resolving the matter and keep an amicable relationship between himself and Philemon as well. In hindsight, the **reason** for which Onesimus was **separated** from Philemon was so that Onesimus could perform a ministry for Paul in Philemon's stead. The details behind the separation are not stated, perhaps to avoid embarrassing Onesimus further and to refrain from reminding Philemon of his loss. While the separation was temporary the return would be permanent since Onesimus has become one of Paul's spiritual children. What is more, on return Onesimus should be received **no longer as a slave but more than a slave, as a beloved brother**. This is the clearest point at which Onesimus's status as a slave is expressed, and the phrase **more than a slave** suggests that his servitude to Philemon is literal rather than metaphorical. The willing return of Onesimus means that he can be received as a dear brother, that is, within the fictive kinship of the Christian movement where brotherly love extends to those who have no grounds for fraternal bonds other than that which unites them under the lordship of Jesus. Although

5. BDAG 229–30.

brotherhood was known as an ideal in the Greek world, such a bond between slaves and masters would have been quite scandalous and viewed as compromising the household order. Treating slaves humanely was not unknown in the Greco-Roman world, but regarding them as brothers would have been viewed as bad for discipline and even self-deprecating for the master (was he to come down to their level?). Slaves born into the household might be fathered by the master through a slave woman and grow up well-educated and cared for alongside legitimate offspring of the master. Sometimes such children were freed and became heirs with well-born children in the household, but even so, for most born into captivity their status as illegitimate slaves would prevent them from ever being legal and social equals with their genetic brothers and sisters of legitimate birth. Perhaps Paul shared the same view held by the Essenes who, according to Philo, denounced slave ownership as it created enmity rather than friendship between human brothers.[6] Paul regards Onesimus as a son and as a brother and the challenge put to Philemon is whether he will imitate Paul's affection towards Onesimus and receive him as a brother.

This appeal, or perhaps better put, this gamble of Paul, is the rhetorical fulcrum on which the epistle turns and a positive outcome is not necessarily assured. How would Philemon respond? He could (1) punish Onesimus for his wrongdoing, (2) restore him to the household and allow him to continue his service as a slave, or (3) manumit Onesimus and send him back to Paul.[7] A mixture of (2) and (3) is what Paul wants. Paul does everything he can to persuade Philemon to accept Onesimus back not as a wayward/runaway slave but as a brother in Messiah, while also intimating his desire to take on Onesimus as a co-worker. The goodness of Philemon and the utility of Onesimus as viewed through the lens of the gospel become the primary motivating forces in the apostle's pastoral rhetoric.

The intensity of Paul's plea for Onesimus is ratcheted up in verses 17–22 with two conditional clauses detailing the depth of Paul's angst over Onesimus's welfare, Philemon's own indebtedness to Paul, and Paul's tacit presumption of Philemon's goodness and hospitality towards him. In the first conditional clause, Paul writes: **If, then, you have partnership with me, receive him as you would receive me.** Here **partnership** means

6. Philo *Prob.* 79.

7. On whether or not Paul makes an implicit plea for Philemon to emancipate Onesimus, see the discussion in Barth and Blanke 2000: 368–69, 412–15.

sharing in one another's affairs in the cause of Jesus Christ. On the one hand, this is an impassioned plea for Philemon to embrace Onesimus as he would Paul, but in another sense it is a gently worded ultimatum to the effect that "if you do not receive him then you do not really have fellowship with me." In the second conditional clause, Paul expresses his willingness to cover any debts incurred by Onesimus's departure: **If he has wronged you, or owes you anything, charge that to me**. Paul is willing to become Philemon's debtor in order to effect reconciliation between the two. It might have been some financial misappropriation, incompetency, or outright theft that marked the occasion of Onesimus's flight to Paul. Paul here says he is willing to pay the debt. He then interjects a very personal remark that **I, Paul, write this with my own hand**, and in effect turns his letter into a promissory note. He emphasizes his willingness to cover any debt with **I will repay it**, underscoring the financial injury suffered to Philemon once more. But the apostle adds, **to say nothing of you owing me your very own self**, which turns Philemon from a creditor into a debtor in the space of two mere verses. The rhetorical function here is of a paralipsis, when a speaker/author asserts that he is passing over something that actually needs to be mentioned. This debt of Philemon to Paul was probably incurred during Philemon's coming to faith. Maybe Paul even "begat" Philemon in much the same way that he has begat Onesimus; in which case Philemon and Onesimus are brothers through having the same spiritual father. This indebtedness to Paul effectively cancels out anything that Onesimus owes Philemon, rendering Paul's offer to financially compensate Philemon as rhetorical. Philemon's indebtedness is emphasized further as Paul says, **Yes, brother, I want some benefit from you in the Lord**. While the affection for Philemon is retained, it is with the implicit qualification that he remains indebted to Paul and should offer up something for Paul's own advantage. Paul was not a social equal to Philemon in the material sense (he owned no property or slaves), but he has nevertheless become Philemon's patron by bringing him the message of salvation. Another play on words is apparent with **benefit** (*oninēmi*) which sounds close to "Onesimus." Paul would like to "benefit" by Philemon as Philemon "benefits" from Onesimus. Philemon, as the client here, is indebted to enhance the honor, advantage, and reputation of his patron and Paul details how. The phrase **Renew my heart in Messiah** harks back to v. 7 where Philemon had reportedly comforted the hearts of the saints in the past and Paul seeks a similar consolation from

Philemon now. The apostle casts the thanksgiving prayer into an imperative. Paul concludes his comments by indicating his confident assurance that Philemon will respond positively to his request to receive Onesimus as a brother. Philemon will hopefully prove obedient in the end, out of love and not compulsion. Paul adds **you will do even more than I ask**, indicating the prospect of Philemon not only receiving Onesimus, but also returning him to Paul's presence. The willingness of Paul to visit Philemon in Colossae marked by **prepare a guest room for me** is hard to reconcile with a Roman provenance and is more believable in an Ephesian setting in the mid to late 50s CE. Paul feels that he can presume upon Philemon's prayers for him and count on a warm reception should he ever visit the location. As Adolf Schlatter commented: "The prayers of the community in its salvation provided Paul with a power from God."[8]

---

8. Schlatter 1987: 322.

PAUL'S FINAL GREETINGS TO PHILEMON (23–25)

> ²³ Epaphras, my fellow prisoner in Messiah Jesus, sends greetings to you, ²⁴ and so do Mark, Aristarchus, Demas, and Luke, my fellow workers. ²⁵ The grace of the Lord Jesus Christ be with your spirit.

Paul's final greeting is very reminiscent of Col 4:10–18 with the same cohort of persons named in both greetings. This is good proof that both letters were written in close proximity to one another and probably from the same location. **Epaphras**, the evangelist and first pastor of the Lycus Valley churches, is mentioned as a **fellow prisoner in Messiah Jesus**, and he may well be attending to Paul's needs under arrest (probably house arrest in a rented room) or perhaps even under detention himself. This is a further ascription of honor to Epaphras and it establishes a closer connection of Epaphras to Paul, which would bolster the standing of Epaphras before the Lycus Valley house churches. Also mentioned is Mark, Aristarchus, Demas, and Luke who are Paul's **fellow workers** for the kingdom. Paul closes with a Christian benediction: **The grace of the Lord Jesus *Christ* be with your spirit**. Importantly, the personal pronoun **your** is in the plural and refers to Philemon's household and the house church as well.

Fusing the Horizons: Ministerial Formation

There are several ways in which the letter to Philemon gives us cause to think about ministerial formation:

1. *The Ministry of Reconciliation.* Central to Paul's theology is the motif of reconciliation.[1] Indeed, some have even argued that this is the central and controlling theme of Pauline theology as a whole.[2] Paul considered his ministry as one of reconciliation (2 Cor 5:18–19), focusing on the breaking down of the sin barrier between God and humanity through the sacrificial death of the Son of God. Paul also saw the barriers between Jews and Gentiles being broken down by the gospel (e.g., Eph 2:14) and could often plead for reconciliation between warring members of Christian congregations (e.g., Phil 4:3). Christians can and should be agents of reconciliation in their ecclesial and social contexts. A large feature of pastoral ministry is the acting out of the message of reconciliation in a community setting. Christians, after all, are called to be peacemakers (Matt 5:9). While not everyone is called to effect reconciliation in places such as post-apartheid South Africa, Northern Ireland, or amidst sectarian violence within the Middle East, still, all Christians are called to promote peace with other human beings and the hope of peace with God through the gospel of Jesus Christ. Since we have been comforted we can comfort others (2 Cor 1:4) and because we have been reconciled to God we can be agents of reconciliation in our churches and in our communities. The act of reconciliation itself can have far reaching effects for society, as Barth and Blanke comment:

> According to Paul's best-known letters, every person, whether Jew or Gentile, needs forgiveness of sins, salvation by Christ's blood rather than self-salvation by the misunderstood and misused law of God, and redemption from eternal death. For everyone the spiritual freedom has immediate consequences in the social setting of his or her own life. But Philem 16 makes it explicit that salvation and redemption, freedom and equality are divine gifts far too precious to be left to the handling of even so good a Christian and so legal a slave owner as Philemon. When this man receives and treats Onesimus as a brother he receives, according to verse 17, a person "sent back" (v. 12) by Paul who is to be received the same way as the apostle hopes to be received. Not only brother Paul but also brother Onesimus will have to show and tell brother Philemon a few things relevant to faith and life, and the latter will have to listen to and follow good advice and proposals. If this be applied to twentieth-century conditions, it means that professional philoso-

1. Cf. discussion in Bird 2008a: 104–6.
2. Cf. recently Marshall 2007: 98–137.

phers and social scientists, pastors and theology professors, politicians and industrial managers, trade unionists and revolutionaries have no monopoly on representing and proclaiming a social order that would deserve to be called free and just and peaceful.[3]

2. *The Ethics of Paul's Pastoral Rhetoric.* On the rhetoric of Paul's letter, it cannot be denied that the epistle is largely emotive and even forceful as it appears to us. This is not a letter from one equal to another, but a superior to an inferior, a teacher to a student, or a mentor to a disciple. Paul gives Philemon a command, but wants him to act out of love not compulsion (vv. 8–9, 14, 21). Paul alleges that Philemon is his debtor and presumes upon his hospitality (vv. 19, 22). The conditional clause of v. 17, "If, then, you have partnership with me, receive him as you would receive me," assumes that Philemon's refusal would mean a rupture in fellowship with Paul. Paul's generosity in verse 18 about covering Onesimus's debt surely presumes upon Philemon's refusal to seek compensation from Paul even as it is offered, and that implies not seeking recompense from Onesimus either. Overall, Paul plays on two motivating principles for persuasion: honor and advantage. Paul anticipates and even celebrates Philemon's compliance before it is promised or even carried out. Thus, if Philemon refuses to acquiesce to Paul's request he then brings dishonor on himself and Paul—dishonor on himself for not living up to the compliments, and on Paul for wrongly bestowing them in the first place. That response would render him thankless and Paul naïve. The advantage that accrues to Philemon is that by obeying he gains Paul's praise and lives up to the accolades stated about him. We should add that this is a private letter communicated before the entire church. Two prominent leaders from Colossae, Archippus and Epaphras, are made aware of the letter, adding further weight to Paul's remarks since their opinion carries weight in the Lycus Valley churches. Philemon's response is eagerly awaited by the entire church to see what he would do as the corporate honor of the assembly is at stake and not merely Philemon's own reputation.

Though this might seem manipulative and even unworthy of an apostle and a Christian minister, I would point out that the contemporary rhetoric of pastoral persuasion is not much different. Imagine a pastor thanking a parishioner for "volunteering" to help out with the annual church picnic when they have not already done so, or writing a group email to the youth leaders confident that they will do the right thing when it comes to cleaning up the

3. Barth and Blanke 2000: 446–47.

auditorium after last night's activities, or perhaps even reminding someone of a charitable act done towards them when a favor needs to be returned. Any ecclesial setting where people need help, direction, and mediation will always necessitate some kind of pastoral persuasion. There can be a fine line between motivation and manipulation. The difference comes down to intent, matters of self-interest, and the vulnerability of persons in question. The ethics of pastoral persuasion are a matter for "practical theology." Suffice to say, in the letter to Philemon, Paul provides an example of how to gently prod persons into doing something that is best for themselves, best for others, and ultimately glorifying of God.

Bibliography

Abbott, T. K. 1897. *Epistles to the Ephesians and to the Colossians*. ICC. Edinburgh: T. & T. Clark.

Ameling, Walter. 2004. *Inscriptiones Judaicae Orientis: II Kleinasien*. TSAJ 99. Tübingen: Mohr/Siebeck.

Arnold, Clinton E. 1996. *The Colossian Syncretism: The Interface Between Christianity and Folk Belief at Colossae*. Grand Rapids: Baker.

Balch, David L. 1981. *Let Wives Be Submissive: The Domestic Code in 1 Peter*. SBLMS 26. Chico, CA: Scholars.

Balla, Peter. 2003. *The Child-Parent Relationship in the New Testament and Its Environment*. WUNT 155. Tübingen: Mohr/Siebeck.

Balz, H. and G. Schneider, editors. 1990. *Exegetical Dictionary of the New Testament*. 3 vols. Grand Rapids: Eerdmans.

Barclay, John M.G. 1997. *Colossians and Philemon*. NTG. Sheffield: Sheffield Academic.

Barth, Markus, and Helmut Blanke. 1994. *Colossians: A New Translation with Introduction and Commentary*. AB 34B. Translated by Astrid B. Beck. New York: Doubleday.

———. 2000. *The Letter to Philemon: A New Translation with Notes and Commentary*. ECC. Grand Rapids: Eerdmans.

Bauckham, Richard. 1975. "Colossians 1:24 Again: The Apocalyptic Motif." *EvQ* 47: 168–70.

———. 1988. "Pseudo-Apostolic Letters." *JBL* 107: 469–94.

Bauer, Walter, Frederick William Danker, William F. Arndt, and F. Wilbur Gingrich. 2000. *A Greek-English Lexicon of the New Testament and Other Early Christian Literature*. 3rd ed. Chicago: University of Chicago Press.

Baur, F. C. [1873–75] 2003. *Paul the Apostle of Jesus Christ: His Life and Works, His Epistles and Teachings*. 2 vols. Peabody, MA: Hendrickson.

Beale, G. K. 2007. "Colossians." In *Commentary on the New Testament Use of the Old Testament*, edited by G. K. Beale and D. A. Carson, 841–70. Grand Rapids: Baker.

Benoit, Pierre. 1968. "Qumran and the New Testament: Paul and Qumran Studies." In *New Testament Exegesis*, edited by Jerome Murphy-O'Connor, 1–30. London: Chapman.

Best, Ernest. 1998. *A Critical and Exegetical Commentary on Ephesians*. ICC. Edinburgh: T. & T. Clark.

Bird, Michael F. 2004. "Mission as an Apocalyptic Event: Reflections on Luke 10:18 and Mark 13:10." *EvQ* 76: 117–34.

———. 2008a. *A Bird's-Eye View of Paul: The Man, His Mission, and His Message*. Nottingham: InterVarsity.

———. 2008b. "Reassessing a Rhetorical Approach to Paul's Letters." *ExpTim* 119: 374–79.

———. Forthcoming. *Crossing Over Sea and Land: Jewish Missionary Activity in the Second Temple Period*. Peabody, MA: Hendrickson.

Bibliography

Blass, F., A. Debrunner, and R. W. Funk, editors. 1961. *A Greek Grammar of the New Testament and Other Early Christian Literature*. 9th ed. Chicago: University of Chicago Press. [BDF]

Blomberg, Craig A. 2003. "Messiah in the New Testament." In *Israel's Messiah in the Bible and the Dead Sea Scrolls*, edited by Richard S. Hess and M. Daniel Carroll R., 111–41. Grand Rapids: Baker.

Bockmuehl, Markus. 1990. *Revelation and Mystery in Ancient Judaism and Pauline Christianity*. WUNT 2.36. Tübingen: Mohr/Siebeck.

Bornkamm, G. 1975. "The Heresy of Colossians." In *Conflict at Colossae: A Problem in the Interpretation of Early Chritiantiy Illustrated by Selected Modern Studies*, edited by W. O. Francis and Wayne A. Meeks, 123–45. Rev. ed. Missoula, MT: Scholars.

Boyd, Gregory A. 2006. "Christus Victor View." In *The Nature of the Atonement: Four Views*, edited by James Beilby and Paul Eddy, 23–49. Downers Grove, IL: InterVarsity.

Bruce, F. F. (with E. K. Simpson). 1957. *Commentary on the Epistles to the Ephesians and the Colossians*. NICNT 12. Grand Rapids: Eerdmans.

———. 1977. *Paul: Apostle of the Heart Set Free*. Grand Rapids: Eeerdmans.

———. 1984a. "Colossian Problem: Part 1: Jews and Christians in the Lycus Valley." *BSac* 141: 3–15.

———. 1984b. "Colossian Problem: Part 2: The 'Christ Hymn' of Colossians 1:15–20." *BSac* 141: 99–111.

———. 1984c. "Colossian Problem: Part 3: The Colossian Heresy." *BSac* 141: 195–208.

———. 1984d. "Colossian Problem: Part 4: Christ as Conqueror and Reconciler." *BSac* 141: 291–302.

Buchegger, Jürg. 2003. *Erneuerung Des Menschen: Exegetische Studien zu Paulus*. Tübingen: Francke.

Bujard, W. 1973. *Stilanalystische Untersuchungen zum Kolosserbrief als Beitrag zur Methodik von Sprachvergleichen*. SUNT 11. Göttingen: Vandenhoeck.

Burk, Denny. 2008. "Is Paul's Gospel Counterimperial? Evaluating the Prospects of the 'Fresh Perspective' for Evangelical Theology." *JETS* 51: 309–37.

Burney, C. F. 1925. "Christ as the APXH of Creation." *JTS* 27: 160–77.

Busch, Peter. 2006. *Magie in neutestamentlicher Zeit*. FRLANT 218. Göttingen: Vandenhoeck & Ruprecht.

Byron, John. 2008. *Recent Research on Paul and Slavery*. Sheffield: Sheffield Phoenix.

Callahan, Allen Dwight. 1993. "Paul's Epistle to Philemon: Towards an Alternative *Argumentum*." *HTR* 86: 357–76.

Calvin, John. 1979a. *Commentaries on the Epistles of Paul the Apostle to the Philippians, Colossians, and Thessalonians*. Translated by John Pringle. Grand Rapids: Eerdmans.

———. 1979b. *Commentaries on the Epistles to Timothy, Titus, and Philemon*. Translated by William Pringle. Grand Rapids: Baker.

Cannon, George E. 1983. *The Use of Traditional Materials in Colossians*. Macon, GA: Mercer University Press.

Charlesworth, James H., editor. 1983, 1985. *Old Testament Pseudepigrapha*. 2 vols. ABRL. New York: Doubleday.

Collins, Raymond F. 2005. *Letters That Paul Did Not Write: The Epistle to the Hebrews and the Pauline Pseudepigrapha*. 1988. Reprinted, Eugene, OR: Wipf & Stock.

"Collosae: Unearthing the Past." N.d. Web site. Flinders University. Online: http://ehlt.flinders.edu.au/theology/institute/colossae/.

Dahl, N. A. 1964. "Christ, Creation and the Church." In *The Background of the New Testament and Its Eschatology*, edited by W. D. Davies and D. Daube, 422–43. Cambridge: Cambridge University Press.

Davies, W. D. 1955. *Paul and Rabbinic Judaism: Some Rabbinic Elements in Pauline Theology*. 2nd ed. London: SPCK.

Deissman, Adolf. 1957. *Paul: A Study in Social and Religious History*. Translated by William E. Wilson. New York: Harper.

———. *Light from the Ancient East*. Translated by L. R. M. Strachan. Peabody, MA: Hendrickson.

DeMaris, Richard E. 1994. *The Colossian Controversy: Wisdom in Dispute at Colossae*. JSNTSup 99. Sheffield: JSOT Press.

deSilva, David A. 2004. *An Introduction to the New Testament: Contexts, Methods and Ministry Formation*. Downers Grove, IL: InterVarsity.

Dibelius, Martin. 1975. "The Isis Initiation in Apuleius and Related Initiatory Rites." In *Conflict at Colossae: A Problem in the Interpretation of Early Chritiantiy Illustrated by Selected Modern Studies*, edited by W. O. Francis and Wayne A. Meeks, 61–121. Missoula, MT: Scholars.

Dunn, James D. G. 1995. "The Colossians Philosophy: A Confident Jewish Apologia." *Bib* 76: 153–81.

———. 1996. *The Epistles to Colossians and to Philemon*. NIGTC. Grand Rapids: Eerdmans.

———. 1998. *The Theology of Paul the Apostle*. Edinburgh: T. & T. Clark.

Ellis, Earle E. 1999. *The Making of the New Testament Documents*. Biblical Interpretation Series 39. Leiden: Brill.

Engberg-Pedersen, Troels. 2000. *Paul and the Stoics*. Philadelphia: Westminster John Knox.

Evans, Craig A. 1982. "The Colossian Mystics." *Bib* 63: 188–205.

Fee, Gordon D. 2007. *Pauline Christology: An Exegetical-Theological Study*. Peabody, MA: Hendrickson.

Fitzmyer, Joseph A. 2000. *The Letter to Philemon: A New Translation with Introduction and Commentary*. AB 34C. New York: Doubleday.

Foster, Robert L. 2008. "Reoriented to the Cosmos: Cosmos and Theology in Ephesians Through Philemon." In *Cosmology and New Testament Theology*, edited by Jonathan T. Pennington and Sean M. McDonough, 107–24. LNTS 355. London: T. & T. Clark.

Francis, Fred O., and Wayne A. Meeks, editors. 1975. *Conflict at Colossae: A Problem in the Interpretation of Early Christianity Illustrated by Selected Modern Studies*. Rev. ed. Missoula, MT: Scholars.

Francis, Fred O. 1975. "Humility and Angelic Worship in Col 2:18." In *Conflict at Colossae: A Problem in the Interpretation of Early Christianity Illustrated by Selected Modern Studies*, edited by Fred O. Francis and Wayne A. Meeks, 163–95. Rev. ed. Missoula, MT: Scholars.

Galling, Kurt, and Hans von Campenhausen, editors. 1957–65. *Religion in Geschichte und Gegenwart*. 7 vols. Tübingen: Mohr/Siebeck.

Garland, David E. 1998. *Colossians and Philemon*. NIVAC. Grand Rapids: Eerdmans.

Gnilka, Joachim. 1980. *Der Kolosserbrief*. Herders theologischer Kommentar zum Neuen Testament 10/1. Freiburg: Herder.

———. 1982. *Der Philemonbrief.* Herders theologischer Kommentar zum Neuen Testament 10/4. Freiburg: Herder.

Gorday, Peter, editor. 2000. *Colossians, 1–2 Thessalonians, 1–2 Timothy, Titus, Philemon.* ACCS 9. Downers Grove, IL: InterVarsity.

Gordley, Matthew E. 2007. *The Colossian Hymn in Context: An Exegesis in Light of Jewish and Greco-Roman Hymnic and Epistolary Conventions.* WUNT 2/228. Tübingen: Mohr/Siebeck.

Gorman, Michael J. 2004. *Apostle of the Crucified Lord: A Theological Introduction to Paul and His Letters.* Grand Rapids: Eerdmans.

Gunther, J. J. 1973. *St. Paul's Opponents and Their Background: A Study of Apocalyptic and Jewish Sectarian Teachings.* NovTSup 35. Leiden: Brill.

Guzlow, H. 1969. *Christentum und Sklaverei in den ersten drei Jahrhunderten.* Bonn: Habelt.

Harrill, J. Albert. 1999. "Using the Roman Jurists to Interpret Philemon." *ZNW* 90: 135–38.

———. 2005. *Slaves in the New Testament: Literary, Social and Moral Dimensions.* Minneapolis: Fortress.

Harris, Murray J. 1991. *Colossians and Philemon.* Exegetical Guide to the Greek New Testament. Grand Rapids: Eerdmans.

Hartman, Lars. 1995. "Code and Context: A Few Reflections on the Parenesis of Col 3:6–4:1." In *"Understanding Paul's Ethics": Twentieth-Century Approaches*, edited by Brian S. Rosner. Grand Rapids: Eerdmans.

Hegermann, Harald. 1961. *Die Vorstellung vom Schöpfungsmittler im hellenistischen Judentum und Urchristentum.* Berlin: Akademie.

Hendriksen, William. 1964. *Colossians and Philemon.* NTC. Edinburgh: Banner of Truth.

Hengel, Martin, and Anna Maria Schwemer. 1997. *Paul between Damascus and Antioch: The Unknown Years.* Translated by John Bowden. London: SCM.

Hentschel, Anni. 2007. *Diakonia im Neuen Testament: Studien zur Semantik unter besonderer Berücksichtigung der Roller von Frauen.* WUNT 2.226. Tübingen: Mohr/Siebeck.

Hooker, Morna D. 1973. "Were There False Teachers in Colossae?" In *Christ and the Spirit in the New Testament*, edited by Barnabas Lindars and S. S. Smalley, 315–31. Cambridge: Cambridge University Press.

Horsley, G. H. R., and S. R. Llewelyn, editors. 1976–87. *New Documents Illustrating Early Christianity.* 9 vols. Grand Rapids: Eerdmans.

Hunt, J. P. T. 1990. "Colossians 2:11–12, the Circumcision/Baptist Analogy, and Infant Baptism." *TynBul* 41: 227–44.

Hurtado, Larry W. 2003. *Lord Jesus Christ: Devotion to Jesus in Earliest Christianity.* Grand Rapids: Eerdmans.

Hvalvik, Reidar. 2005. "All Those Who in Every Place Call on the Name of Our Lord Jesus Christ." In *The Formation of the Early Church*, edited by Jostein Ådna, 123–43. WUNT 183; Tübingen: Mohr/Siebeck.

Jewett, Robert. 1979. *A Chronology of Paul's Life.* Philadelphia: Fortress.

Käsemann, Ernst. 1964. "A Primitive Christian Baptismal Liturgy." In *Essays on New Testament Themes*, 149–68. Translated by W. J. Montague. SBT 1/41. London: SCM.

Keck, Leander E. 1988. *Paul and His Letters.* 2nd ed. PC. Philadelphia: Fortress.

Kee, Howard Clark. 2005. *The Beginnings of Christianity: An Introduction to the New Testament.* New York: T. & T. Clark.

Keener, Craig S. 1992. *Paul, Women, and Wives: Marriage and Women's Ministry in the Letters of Paul.* Peabody, MA: Hendrickson.

Kiley, Mark. 1986. *Colossians as Pseudepigraphy.* Biblical Seminar 4. Sheffield: JSOT Press.

Kim, Seyoon. 2008. *Christ and Caesar: The Gospel and the Roman Empire in the Writings of Paul and Luke.* Grand Rapids: Eerdmans.

Kittel, Gerhard, and Gerhard Friedrich, editors. 1964–1976. *Theological Dictionary of the New Testament.* Translated by G. W. Bromiley. 10 vols. Grand Rapids: Eerdmans.

Knox, John. 1950. *Chapters in a Life of Paul.* New York: Abingdon.

———. 1959. *Philemon among the Letters of Paul: A New View of Its Place and Importance.* New York: Abingdon.

Knox, W. L. 1939. *St Paul and the Church of the Gentiles.* Cambridge: Cambridge University Press.

Kooten, Geurt Hendrik van. 2003. *Cosmic Christology in Paul and the Pauline School: Colossians and Ephesians in the Context of Graeco-Roman Cosmology, with a New Synopsis of the Greek Texts.* WUNT 2/171. Tübingen: Mohr/Siebeck.

Kümmel, W. G. 1975. *Introduction to the New Testament.* Translated by Paul Feine. Nashville: Abingdon.

Lightfoot, J. B. 1879. *Saint Paul's Epistles to the Colossians and to Philemon.* 3rd ed. London: Macmillan.

Lincoln, Andrew T. 2000. *The Letter to the Colossians.* In *NIB* 11: 551–669. Nashville: Abingdon.

Lohse, Eduard. 1971. *Colossians and Philemon.* Translated by William R. Poehlmann and Robert J. Karris. Hermeneia. Philadelphia: Fortress.

Lucas, Dick. 1980. *The Message of Colossians & Philemon: Fullness and Freedom.* BST. Downers Grove, IL: InterVarsity.

Lüdemann, Gerd. 1984. *Paul, Apostle to the Gentiles: Studies in Chronology.* Translated by F. Stanley Jones. Philadelphia: Fortress.

MacDonald, Margaret Y. 2005. "Can Nympha Rule This House? The Rhetoric of Domesticity in Colossians." In *Rhetoric and Reality in Early Christianities*, edited by Willi Braun, 99–120. ESCJ 16. Waterloo, ON: Wilfrid Laurier University Press.

———. 2008. *Colossians, Ephesians.* SP 17. Collegeville, MN: Liturgical.

Maier, Harry O. 2005. "A Sly Civility: Colossians and Empire." *JSNT* 27: 323–49.

Marshall, I. Howard. 2007. *Aspects of Atonement: Cross and Resurrection in the Reconciling of God and Humanity.* Milton Keynes, UK: Paternoster.

Martin, Ralph P. 1973. *Colossians and Philemon.* NCB. London: Marshall, Morgan & Scott.

Martin, Troy W. 1996. *By Philosophy and Empty Deceit: Colossians as Response to a Cynic Critique.* JSNTSup 118. Sheffield: JSOT Press.

McKnight, Scot. 2007. *A Community Called Atonement.* Nashville: Abingdon.

Mead, David G. 1986. *Pseudonymity and Canon: An Investigation into the Relationship of Authorship and Authority in Jewish and Earliest Christian Traditions.* WUNT 39. Tübingen: Mohr/Siebeck.

Metzger, Bruce M. 1994. *A Textual Commentary on the Greek New Testament.* 2nd ed. Stuttgart: Deutsche Bibelgesellschaft/United Bible Societies.

Meyer, Marvin, and Richard Smith. 1994. *Ancient Christian Magic: Coptic Texts of Ritual Power*. San Francisco: Harper.

Moule, C. F. D. 1957. *The Epistles of Paul to the Colossians and to Philemon*. CGTC. Cambridge: Cambridge University Press.

———. 1973. "'The New Life' in Colossians 3:1–17." *RevExp* 70: 481–93.

O'Brien, Peter T. 1982. *Colossians, Philemon*. WBC 44. Waco, TX: Word.

O'Donnell, Matthew Brooks. 2005. *Corpus Linguistics and the Greek of the New Testament*. NTM 6. Sheffield: Sheffield Phoenix.

Petersen, *Norman R.* 1985. *Rediscovering Paul: Philemon and the Sociology of Paul's Narrative World*. Reprinted, Eugene, OR: Wipf & Stock, 2008.

Pizzuto, Vincent. 2006. *A Cosmic Leap of Faith: An Authorial, Structural, and Theological Investigation of the Cosmic Christology in Col 1:15–20*. Leuven: Peeters.

Pokorný, Petr. 1991. *Colossians: A Commentary*. Translated by S. S. Schatzmann. Peabody, MA: Hendrickson.

Porter, Stanley E. 1994. *Idioms of the Greek New Testament*. 2nd ed. Sheffield: Sheffield Academic.

Reicke, Bo Ivar. 2001. *Re-examining Paul's Letters: The History of the Pauline Correspondence*, edited by David P. Moessner and Ingalisa Reicke. Harrisburg, PA: Trinity.

Richard, Earl J. 1988. *Jesus, One and Many: The Christological Concept of New Testament Authors*. Wilmington, DE: Glazier.

Riesner, Rainer. 1998. *Paul's Early Period: Chronology, Mission Strategy, Theology*. Grand Rapids: Eerdmans.

Roberts, J. H. 1998. "Jewish Mystical Experience in the Early Christian Era as Background to Understanding Colossians." *NeoT* 32: 161–89.

Rowland, Christopher. 1983. "Apocalyptic Visions and the Exaltation of Christ in the Letter to the Colossians." *JSNT* 19: 73–83.

Sappington, Thomas J. 1991. *Revelation and Redemption at Colossae*. JSNTSup 53. Sheffield: JSOT Press.

Schlatter, Adolf. 1909. "Die Theologie Des Neuen Testaments und die Dogmatik." *Beitrag Zur Forderung Christlicher Theologie* 13: 7–82.

———. 1987. *Die Briefe an die Galater, Epheser, Kolosser und Philemon*. Stuttgart: Calwer.

Schüssler Fiorenza, Elisabeth. 1983. *In Memory of Her: A Feminist Theological Reconstruction of Christian Origins*. New York: Crossroad.

Schweizer, Eduard. 1982. *The Letter to the Colossians*. Translated by Andrew Chester. London: SPCK.

Scott, E. F. 1930. *The Epistles of Paul to the Colossians, to Philemon, and to the Ephesians*. MNTC. London: Hodder & Stoughton.

Smith, Ian K. 2006. *Heavenly Perspective: A Study of the Apostle Paul's Response to a Jewish Mystical Movement at Colossae*. LNTS 326. London: T. & T. Clark.

Stettler, Christian. 2000. *Der Kolosserhymnus: Untersuchungen zu Form, Traditionsgeschichtlichem Hintergrund und Aussage von Kol 1,15–20*. WUNT 2/131. Tübingen: Mohr/Siebeck.

———. 2005. "The Opponents at Colossae." In *Paul and His Opponents*, edited by Stanley E. Porter, 169–200. PSt 2. Leiden: Brill.

Stettler, Hanna. 2000. "An Interpretation of Colossians 1:24 in the Framework of Paul's Mission Theology." In *The Mission of the Early Church to Jews and Gentiles*, edited by Jostein Ådna and Hans Kvalbein, 185–208. WUNT 127. Tübingen: Mohr/Siebeck.

Still, Todd D. 2004. "Eschatology in Colossians: How Realized Is It?" *NTS* 50: 125–38.

Stuckenbruck, Loren. 1995. *Angel Veneration and Christology: A Study in Early Judaism and in the Christology of the Apocalypse of John.* WUNT 2/70. Tübingen: Mohr/Siebeck.

———. 2003. "Colossians and Philemon." In *The Cambridge Companion to St. Paul,* edited by James D. G. Dunn, 116–32. Cambridge: Cambridge University Press.

Sumney, Jerry. 1993. "Those Who 'Pass Judgment': The Identity of Paul's Opponents in Colossians." *Bib* 74: 366–68.

Talbert, Charles H. 2007. *Ephesians and Colossians.* Paideia. Grand Rapids: Baker.

Tamez, Elsa. 2007. *Struggles for Power in Early Christianity.* Translated by Gloria Kinsler. Maryknoll, NY: Orbis.

Thielman, Frank. 2003. "Ephesus and the Literary Setting of Philippians." In *New Testament Greek and Exegesis: Essays in Honor of Gerald B. Hawthorne,* edited by Amy M. Donaldson and Timothy B. Sailors, 205–23. Grand Rapids: Eerdmans.

Thompson, Marianne Meye. 2005. *Colossians and Philemon.* TH. Grand Rapids: Eerdmans.

Thompson, Michael B. 1998. "The Holy Internet: Communication between Churches in the First Christian Generation." In *The Gospels for All Christians: Rethinking the Gospel Audiences,* edited by R. Bauckham, 49–70. Grand Rapids: Eerdmans.

Trebilco, Paul R. 1991. *Jewish Communities in Asia Minor.* Cambridge: Cambridge University Press.

———. 2006. "'Global' and 'Local' in the New Testament and in Earliest Christianity." Inaugural professorial lecture, University of Otago.

Wall, Robert W. 1993. *Colossians and Philemon.* IVPNTC. Downers Grove, IL: InterVarsity.

Walsh, Brian J., and Sylvia J. Keesmaat. 2004. *Colossians Remixed: Subverting the Empire.* Downers Grove, IL: InterVarsity.

Watson, Francis. 2007. *Paul, Judaism, and the Gentiles: Beyond the New Perspective.* Grand Rapids: Eerdmans.

Wedderburn, A. J. M. 1987. *Baptism and Resurrection: Studies in Pauline Theology against Its Graeco-Roman Background.* WUNT 44. Tübingen: Mohr/Siebeck.

Wenham, David. 1995. *Follower of Jesus or Founder of Christianity?* Grand Rapids: Eerdmans.

Williams, David J. 1999. *Paul's Metaphors: Their Character and Context.* Peabody, MA: Hendrickson.

Wilson, R. McL. 2005. *Colossians and Philemon.* ICC. London: T. & T. Clark.

Winter, Sarah C. 1987. "Paul's Letter to Philemon." *NTS* 33: 1–15.

Witherington, Ben III. 2007. *The Letters to Philemon, the Colossians, and the Ephesians: A Socio-Rhetorical Commentary on the Captivity Epistles.* Grand Rapids: Baker.

Wolter, M. 1993. *Der Brief an die Kolosser. Der Brief an Philemon.* ÖTKNT 12. Gütersloh: Mohn.

Wright, N. T. 1991. *The Climax of the Covenant: Christ and the Law in Pauline Theology.* Edinburgh: T. & T. Clark.

———. 1986. *Colossians and Philemon.* TNTC. Grand Rapids: Eerdmans.

———. 2005. *Paul: Fresh Perspectives.* London: SPCK.

Yamauchi, Edwin. 1964. "Sectarian Parallels: Qumran and Colossae." *BSac* 121: 141–52.

Name Index

Scripture Index

APOCRYPHA

Scripture Index

OTHER CHRISTIAN WRITINGS

GRECO-ROMAN AUTHORS